MICROSOFT

WORD 2021

FOR BEGINNERS & POWER USERS

The Concise Microsoft Office Word
A-Z Mastery Guide for All Users

D1716366

Tech Demystified

ISBN: 9798504074405

CONTENTS

INTRODUCTION

Microsoft Word 2019 has been the latest version of Microsoft Office Suite, not only the latest version but the "come to stay" version where periodically it can be fully monitored and updated without any threat of software crash or unauthorized version. With Word 2019, you have limitless access to Microsoft's subsequent features such as frequent updates from Microsoft, One Drive cloud storage, personal email to validate your identification, the opportunity to make use of other Microsoft products, and lots more.

From time past till date, Word has been the undefeated Word Processor text editor that is not only limited to typing, no wonder companies can't do without it, schools keep educating pupils about it and some take it as a life coaching opportunity due to the lack of thorough understanding about it.

I am challenging you today, for those who are thinking maybe this is one of the usual handbooks, and for others who are doubting the credibility of this powerful practical guide. A book should not be judged by its cover until the content has been revealed. Many testimonies have been coming in concerning this practical guide and yours can't be the last. This is not a practical guide on what might be outdated in the long run but what will continuously be relevant.

This is a guide that does not only explain "WHAT" (theoretical application), but also "HOW" (practical application). I am excited because you have just made the right choice.

Please, note that this user guide is applicable to both Office 365 and Office 2019 users. You can easily deploy the knowledge gained by reading this book to effectively make use word with office 365 subscriptions. See you in the next section!

CHAPTER ONE

OFFICE NUTS & BOLTS

Introduction to Office 2021

In the past, Microsoft Office was always sold as box software, so when you buy your new computer, you have the options of buying Office whether Microsoft Office 2007, 2010, 2013, 2016 or other subsequent versions. You could pay $300USD to $500USD depending on the version you request for, and you will get the software on your machine which would be installed into your PC as infinity software, meaning you will pay once and never pay again for the software, this is how Microsoft deals with its previous products for very long time.

In the past several years, many companies have started switching over to a subscription model of selling software such as Adobe, Photoshop, and other subscription software; you can't just buy them completely anymore. You purchase a subscription and through that subscription, you always get the latest updated and upgraded version of any other program you subscribe for. So, with Microsoft, they sell box software which also leads to an upgrade in its service rendering for a quick solution to unexpected issues, flexible storage space, and secured information with other benefits only available to its subscribed users.

Historical Background of Microsoft Word

- *Microsoft Word DOS:* The first version of Microsoft Word was released in 1983, it was named Microsoft Word DOS which stands for "Disk Operating System", with a 16bit system type capacity.
- *Microsoft Word for Windows:* Another version of Microsoft Word was released in 1989 with a different edition.

- *Microsoft **Word 95:*** After the release of Microsoft Word for Windows which had a lot of limitations, Microsoft Word 95 was released in 1995 to solve the problem of graphics and limited features.
- *Microsoft **Word 97:*** Microsoft Word 97 was released on November 19, 1996, to solve the limitation of Microsoft Word 95.
- *Microsoft **Word 2000:*** Microsoft Word 97 was replaced by Microsoft Word 2000 as a new release on July 7, 1999.
- *Microsoft **Word 2001/Word X:*** Word 2001 was packaged with the Macintosh features. Word 2001 was released in October 2000 and was also sold as an individual product. Word X was released in 2001 and was the first version to run natively
- *Microsoft **Word 2002/XP:*** Word 2002 was also released in 2001 to replace Microsoft Word 2001 & Word X. It had several of the same features as Word 2000, but a new feature was added called the "Task Panes", which gave quicker information and control to a lot of features.
- *Microsoft **Word 2003:*** Microsoft Word 2003 is an office suite developed by Microsoft for its Windows operating system. Office 2003 was released on October 21, 2003. It was the replacement of Word XP.
- *Microsoft **Word 2007:*** Word 2007 was introduced with a graphical user interface called the "Fluent User Interface", ribbons and an Office menu. It was released on January 30, 2007.
- *Microsoft **Word 2010:*** Microsoft Word 2010 is another version of the Microsoft Office suite for Microsoft Windows. Office 2010 was released on the 15th of April 2010. It is the successor to Word 2007.
- *Microsoft **Word 2013:*** Word 2013 was released on January 29, 2013, with more updated features and was later replaced by Word 2016

- ***Microsoft Word 2016:*** Word 2016 was launched on September 22, 2015, with a lot of built-in features such as auto-correct, spelling check, auto-save, and lots more. Word 2016 was later replaced with Word 2019.
- ***Microsoft Word 2019:*** Word 2019 was released on September 24, 2018, with similar yet upgraded features such as Sign in, share, and auto-resume with other friendly tools. It was later replaced with Word 2019.
- ***Microsoft Word 2019:*** Word 2019 was released on June 28, 2011, with a similar interface yet different with newly added features such as speech dictation, resume assistant, sharing of documents online, OneDrive cloud storage, and lots more. Word 2019 is the latest version of Microsoft Word which functions online; without having a Microsoft account you are not eligible to make use of it.

What is Office 2021 Cloud Service?

Office 2019 is a collection of different cloud applications which serve different purposes but similar in features. It is important to note that Office 2019 has been synchronized as Microsoft 2021 which comes with many packages such as:

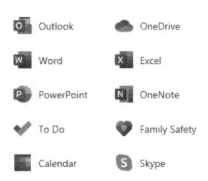

- **Word:** It is a text editor specifically designed to process text, image, shapes & other features without the need to manually install it on your PC.

- **Excel:** This is a calculation framed software used to solve the complexity of statistics, Mathematics, and plotting of graphs with other features in a flexible way.
- **PowerPoint:** It is the software majorly constructed for presentation purposes.
- **Outlook:** Outlook is an email that is designed to receive incoming messages and also send outgoing messages.
- **OneDrive**: This is an online storage space specifically designed for all Microsoft users to store personal data which can be accessed anywhere around the world. It also comes with a link privilege to share files and other items stored on it.
- **OneNote:** OneNote is a note-taking software
- **To Do:** It is a task management utility that is designed to take your regular activities schedule.
- **Family Safety:** This is also another feature of Microsoft that gives the privilege to monitor your family activities such as setting screen time limits, filtering of content, activities report, and lots more to make sure family members are safe while using the internet with Microsoft.
- **Calendar:** It is used to schedule and share meetings and event times. One can automatically get reminders.
- **Skype:** This is a meeting software which is designed to make video and voice call, chat and share file or screen if need be.

Difference between Office 365 & Microsoft 2019

Office 365 is a cloud-based software collection of applications such as Word, Excel, PowerPoint, and more. Microsoft 2019 is a bundle of existing services under one license that includes Office 2019 with several other services including Windows 10 Enterprise plus Security tools. Sooner or later, Microsoft will be branding its cloud-based productivity suite, Office 2019, as Microsoft 2019. This amendment in the naming resolution reflects Microsoft's strategy to convert all its products & services under one common name to avoid any confusion among its users by bringing everything under one umbrella.

Types of Microsoft Office 2019 Suite

For every Microsoft product and service, there is always an avenue for multiple choice for users. Microsoft Office 2019 suite is divided into two categories:

Microsoft Office 2019 Subscription Plans	Description
• **Home Plans** Family Personal	• Microsoft 2019 **Family** costs $95USD to $100USD per year for 2 to 6 people with 1 Terabyte (TB) storage per person. • Microsoft 2019 **Personal** costs $60USD to $65USD. Only per year package is available for 1 person with 1 Terabyte (TB) storage Both plans give access to Microsoft Office applications such as Word, Excel, PowerPoint, OneDrive, 60mins Skype per month, and more.
• **Business Plans** Business Basic Business Standard Business Premium Apps for business	• Microsoft 2019 **Business Basic** costs $5 per month with access to Office suite packages • Microsoft 2019 **Business Standard** costs $12.50 per month with access to Office suite packages • Microsoft 2019 **Business Premium** costs $20USD user per month with access to Office suite packages

	• Microsoft 2019 **Apps for Business** costs $8.25USD per month. It is best for businesses that need easy remote solutions, with Microsoft Teams, secured cloud storage, and Office Online. The business plan includes a 300-user limit. Packages are a little different from one another depending on your need.
• **Enterprise Plans** Enterprise 3 Enterprise 5 Firstline 3 Apps for Enterprise	• Microsoft 2019 E3 costs $32USD per month • Microsoft 2019 E5 price is not fixed • Microsoft 2019 F3 costs $8USD per month Enterprise plan includes unlimited user features. All these prices might vary depending on your country's currency and Microsoft update of other features which might affect the price.

Note

i. **Microsoft 2019 for home plans:** are for family usage which gives room for monitoring of family members' activities for the sake of children.

ii. **Microsoft 2019 for business plans:** are mainly for organizational usage. It is designed to suit office performances and is also used to secure remote work.

iii. **Microsoft 2019 for enterprise plans:** This is similar to the business plan but different in some aspects, enterprise plan gives the privilege

Why should I use Office 2021 over previous versions?

It is important to note that the world at large is moving fast beyond human imagination, just as we have our daily experience so also is the advancement of technology moving rapidly.

Over time, Microsoft has found it a bit difficult to release an update on the purchased version since all previous versions of Suite majorly work offline; auto-update will be difficult or impossible to occur to them all

from Office 2007, Office 2010, Office 2013, Office 2016 to Office 2019. Microsoft users find it a waste of time to update since everything is working perfectly, which led to the latest version which is online-based known as Office 2019. It's a cloud service that works directly from the Microsoft database for security and monitoring purposes. Very soon application installation won't relent any longer due to the rate of technology advancement daily.

Becoming a Microsoft User

Many people find it difficult to create an account with Microsoft, which without an account you can't enjoy the limitless benefits of Microsoft features. Below are steps on how to go about it

- Go to your browser search for **"Microsoft office 2019",** make sure it is Microsoft link then click on **"Official Microsoft 2019® Site - Formerly Office 2019®"**

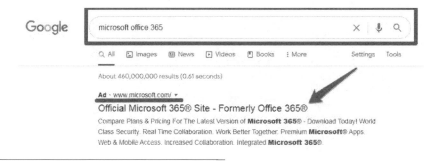

- You will be brought into the Microsoft website, below is a link to **"Sign in",** click on it or you can also locate an image icon at your top right-hand side, you can also click on it

- Or you can directly type Microsoft website into your browser www.microsoft.com. Once the Microsoft website is done loading, look at your right-hand side you will see **an image icon,** click on it to create your user account

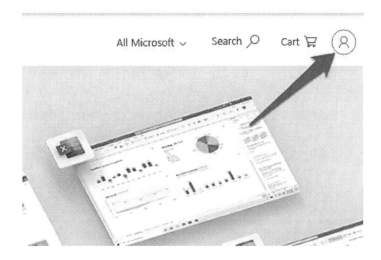

- You will be brought here, simply enter your existing Microsoft account. If you don't have one click on **"Create One".**

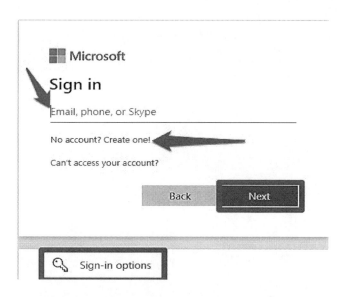

- In case you can't access your account, click on **"Can't access your account"** below create one, a dialog box will appear notifying you that your Windows 10 operating system will receive a security key that will give you access

- Or you want a sign-in option without you having to enter your password for reasons best known to you, simply click on **"Sign-in options"**

- If none of these is your case but want to create an account simply click on **"Create one"**

- Simply follow the instructions to get your Microsoft account opened, once done, you will be brought into Microsoft 2019 environment

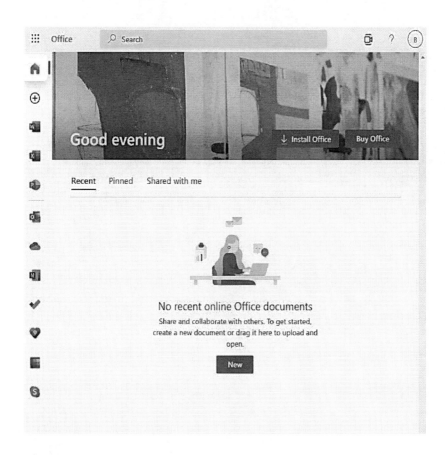

CHAPTER TWO
WELCOME TO WORD 2021

Word 2021 Installed License Environment

Word 2021 Free Web based Environment

Word 2019 interface is designed to perform similar tasks as previous versions with more added features such as online help, latest release, online sharing, and lots more.

Exploring Word 2019

For simplicity and comprehension, I will be using the free web version to explain Word 2019 features for the sake of those who can't afford a license version yet, and for those that can, I will be using both to explain along the line to be able to cover both parts.

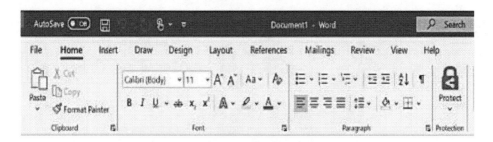

Word 2019 comes with simple yet loaded features that autosave itself online into your OneDrive cloud storage

Title bar functionality

The title bar consists of your application name which is **"Word"** and beside it is your current working document which can be renamed, and also the location of your document storage which is OneDrive as seen above.

Exploring tab Functionality

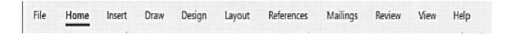

A menu bar is the anchor or entry point that leads to other features. The menu bar names details where you can access such features from:

File tab features

Once you click on "file", it'll display a dialog box that gives an overview of multiple features of what **"File menu"** represent.

Home: Home under **"File menu"** also known as the **"backstage view"** takes you to Word 2019 launching page where you can open a new document to work on, locate existing documents and also see your recent works.

Home

New

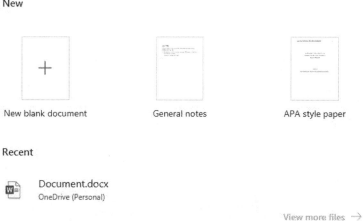

New blank document   General notes   APA style paper

Recent

Document.docx
OneDrive (Personal)

View more files →

Info: Info gives the privilege to make use of previous Microsoft Word on your desktop or PC, Protection view and to view, restore or download previous versions of your document.

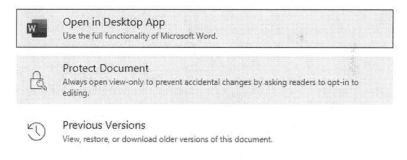

Info

	Open in Desktop App
W	Use the full functionality of Microsoft Word.

Protect Document
Always open view-only to prevent accidental changes by asking readers to opt-in to editing.

Previous Versions
View, restore, or download older versions of this document.

Save as: This is the feature that makes Microsoft Word 2019 save & rename an active document because there is no save button, every work is automatically saved online. You can also click on **"Download a copy"** to download a duplicate copy into your PC, or **"Download as PDF"** directly into your PC, or **"Download as ODT"** to your PC.

Save as

Where's the Save Button?

There's no Save button because we're automatically saving your document.

Export: Export gives room for transferring a document into another Microsoft 2019 Suite such as PowerPoint. As time goes on, more options will be added to the list.

Export

Export to PowerPoint presentation (preview)
Export your document into a multi-slide presentation with a design theme.

Print: The print option is designed to covert softcopy into hardcopy format, all that is needed is a connected printer to complete this process of printing.

Print

Share: This is the feature that allows you to share your document with others by inviting them, and you can also embed this document in your blog or website

---

16

Share

About: The about option gives the summary of terms and conditions of using Word 2019 with third-party notice. Under the about option is where you get your product ID known as "Session ID", and "Build" for any technical support from Microsoft.

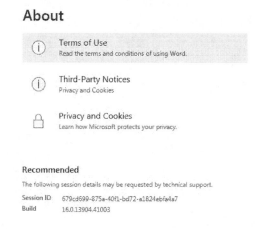

Home tab feature

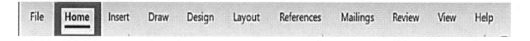

"Home" as its name implies, is the default displayed feature of the Word 2019 interface which comes with ribbons that are grouped for your command, these can also be categorized as ***Standard toolbar*** for customizing your text and ***formatting toolbar*** for editing your text. Home comes with tools for beautifying text such as:

- **Clipboard ribbon tab:** Clipboard is one of Microsoft tool designed as part of Word 2019 to cut, copy and paste an item

- **Cut:** Cut removes a selected portion and stores it directly into your clipboard.
- **Copy:** Copy duplicates item and stores it into your clipboard.
- **Format Painter:** This is a tool used to duplicate a text format into another text format.
- **Paste:** Paste displays all cut or copied items to any assigned destination.
- **Font ribbon tab:** Font is a Word 2019 ribbon that consists of various tools for editing your text font style, font size, superscript, subscript, color, and lots more.

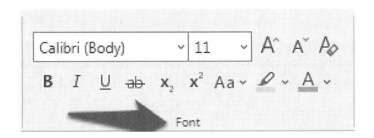

- **Bold:** It is a tool that makes your text appear in a bold form, it is recognized by a bold **B** icon
- **Italic:** It is a tool that slants or slopes your text, it is recognized by a slant "*I*" icon
- **Underline:** It is a tool that rules a line under a selected text, it is recognized by an underlined U icon
- **Strikethrough:** It is a tool used to cross through your text, it is recognized by a strikethrough ab̶ icon

- **Font style:** It is designed to beautify text style into your preferred choice.

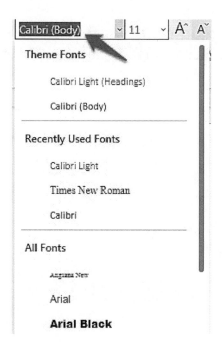

- *Font size:* This is another portion that gives increment and decrement to your text.

- *Font Color:* It is the tool that changes the color of your text into your preferred choice, it affects the selected text body. It is represented with a capital letter A underlined with red color.

- *Text highlighted color:* This is similar to font color. Text highlighted color affects highlighted text background areas. It is represented with a pen icon underlined with yellow color.

- ***Superscript & Subscript:*** This is the feature responsible for text positioning, superscript makes text above the text line, while subscript makes text below the text line.

- ***Change Case:*** It is a feature that gives the privilege to change text into lowercase, uppercase, sentence case, and other formats, it is represented with capital letter A and a small letter 'a' (Aa)

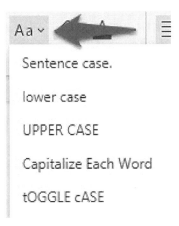

- ***Clear formatting:*** This helps to remove all formatting from the selection, leaving only the normal text unformatted. It is represented as seen in the illustration below

- **Paragraph ribbon tab:** "Paragraph" is a ribbon tab that other commands are grouped into for specialization. Paragraph features are also known as formatting toolbar for aligning text in an orderly approach. Part of paragraph features are:

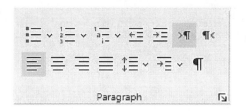

- **Bullet's library:** Bullets is a tagged icon that works in form of numerical numbering. In bullets, every symbol icon is the same in listing except there is a need to have sub-list items

- **Numbering library:** Numbering is the opposite of bullets. Numbering comes in forms, numerical order, alphabetical order, and roman figure order

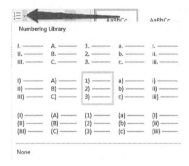

- **Multilevel library:** It is a sub-listing arrangement that consists of a mixture of bullets listing & numbering listing in sublevels.

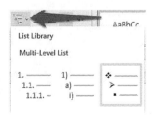

- ***Decrease & Increase Indent:*** It is designed to adjust the movement of text from a standpoint to another standpoint.

- ***Left-to-right text direction:*** This is an auto feature that moves an item from the left-hand side position to the right-hand side

- ***Right-to-left text direction:*** It is the opposite of the left-to-right text direction. It automatically moves text from the right-hand side position to the left-hand side position

- ***Left alignment:*** It helps to align your content to the left margin

- ***Center alignment:*** It helps to centralize your content
- ***Right alignment:*** It helps to align your content to the right margin
- ***Justify alignment:*** It helps your content to look fit on right and left margin
- ***Line spacing:*** This is another feature of the paragraph ribbon tab. Line spacing determines the space between lines of text or between paragraphs.

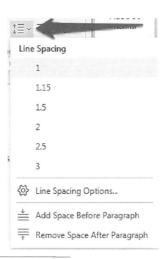

- **Styles:** Style gives your content a consistent polish look. It also comes with multiple options to choose from through the navigation pane

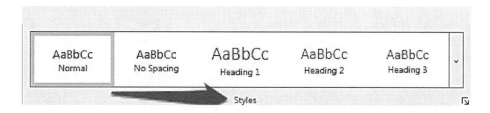

- **Editing:** Editing is a tool that is used to find text, replace text, and also to select text

- **Dictate:** Dictate is a new tool added into Word 2019 that allows its users the privilege to use speech-to-text.

- **Editor:** Editor is a tool in Word 2019 that offers auto spelling & grammar suggestions.

- **Designer:** Designer is a newly added tool that presents a list of potential features for fonts and headings that you can apply to your document to make it professionally presentable. It also gives users the privilege to professionally design complete templates

Designer

Insert tab feature

Insert menu bar feature is designed to add, import & customize your content in a lovely way. Insert menu bar has many tools such as:

- **Pages ribbon tab:** This is the controller of your contents, that involves page breaks. Subsequent updates from Microsoft will lead to additional features such as cover page and others.

- **Table ribbon tab:** The table ribbon tab is responsible for table creation based on your preferred choice

- **Picture ribbon tab:** It is a tool that grants access to images from external images on your PC into Word 2019 environment.

- **Add-ins ribbon tab:** Add-in is a feature that allows Microsoft users to merge external application features with Word 2019

- **Link ribbon tab:** Link makes it possible for link creation into another file, webpage, and lots more.

- **Comments ribbon tab:** This is a feature that adds a note on a selected text, majorly for reference purpose

- **Header & Footer:** "Header" helps you to repeat content at the top of every page while "footer" helps you to repeat content at the bottom of every page.

- **Symbols ribbon tab:** Symbol comes with various mathematical representations that can be used for different purposes based on the user's preferred choice.

- **Emoji ribbon tab:** Emoji is a newly added feature that is still under development. Emoji is a little facial expression image that was first recognized on smartphones. Microsoft is bringing the possibility of Word 2019 emoji.

Note: More features are being updated daily with time, and there will be lesser usage of offline Word application once Microsoft stops it support from previous versions.

Design tab features

The design tab is an embodiment of document formatting tools and page background styling such as:

- **Document Formatting ribbon tab:** It is a group collection of tools for styling your document
  - **Themes:** This is a feature that enables a predefined template format for styling your document content from a professional viewpoint.

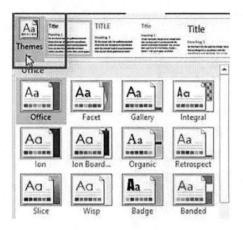

- **Colors:** Microsoft Word predefined templates also come with redefining colors for an individual preferred choice.

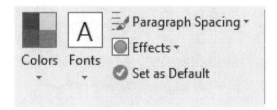

- **Fonts:** Microsoft also comes with a lot of fonts that can sort your preferred choice since individual taste varies. With this, you can redefine your theme font.
- **Page Background ribbon tab:** It is a group of collections used to edit your theme template and also to customize your pages.

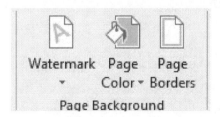

- **Watermark:** Watermark is a great tool used to design your background document with either a text or image depending on the individual preferred choice.

- **Page Color:** This helps you to customize your page document from the default white color to another color of your choice.
- **Page Borders:** It is used to create a variety of line styles, widths, and colors.

Layout tab feature

Layout is Word 2019 menu bar that is responsible for page settings such as:

- **Page Setup ribbon tab:** This is the ribbon tab that groups other commands responsible for page configuration such as:

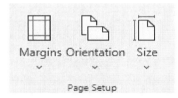

  - **Margins:** It is used to set the right and left edge for all pages, it is a manual page setting.
  - **Orientation:** Page orientation is divided into two categories, portrait & landscape; by default, your Word settings is on portrait, the landscape is used for different purposes such as tabulation of analysis.
  - **Size:** Page size helps to make use of different paper sizes such as A4 (which is Word default paper size), A5, and many more. It is an auto page setting.

- **Paragraph ribbon tab:** This is a manual setup for paragraph settings, it is used to set indent and space.

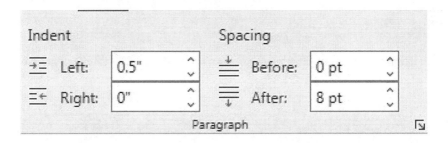

- **Left & Right Indent:** They both determine how far to move the paragraph away from the left margin and the right margin.
- **Before & After Spacing:** They both determine how much space appears above or below the selected paragraph.

References menu bar:

The references menu bar consists of different Word 2019 tools such as Updating table of contents, Footnotes, and Insights

- **Table of Contents ribbon tab:** This is used for the arrangement of contents.
- **Footnote ribbon tab:** Is used to take note for citation of written words.
    - **Update Table of Contents:** Word 2019 provides an overview of your document by adding a table of content
    - **Remove Table of Contents:** You can auto-remove your created table of contents at your wish
- **Footnotes ribbon tab:** Footnote is a written text on the bottom of Word 2019 page to reference a sentence; it is majorly used for journals.
- **Insights ribbon tab:** This is a newly added feature that serves as a mini browser to get an insight into a word or statement.

Review tab:

The review menu bar is designed to give a comprehensive detail on your written document such as:

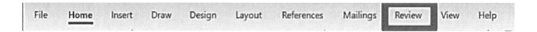

- **Editor ribbon tab:** It is a tool used to check spellings and correct words.

- **Word Count ribbon tab:** It is a tool designed to auto count words & pages.

- **Accessibility ribbon tab:** The Accessibility feature helps to verify your document against a set of instructions that detect possible issues for people who have disabilities. Depending on how severe the issue is, the Accessibility Checker classifies each issue as an error, warning, or tip.

- **Translate ribbon tab:** The Translate feature is a tool that helps you to interpret text into a different language. By using Word 2019 you are already connected online to get your translated words.

- **Comments ribbon tab:** It helps to add a note about any selected part of your content and also, other tools reveal your comment items

- **Tracking ribbon tab:** Tracking helps you to keep in touch with your document in case of any changes made by you or other people you shared your document with. It is majorly used to note every single step of added and removed words.

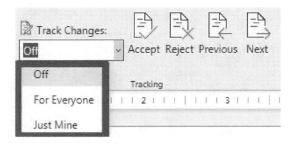

- **Resume Assistant:** It is a newly added feature from Microsoft Word 2019 that enables its users to get different templates.

Resume Assistant

Mailing's tab

Mailing's tab is a feature used to forward, edit, and select emails.

View tab

The view menu bar is constructed to preview content, read content, zoom in & out, and lots more

- **Document Views ribbon tab:** This is a new feature added into Word 2019 where you can view your content and also make your PC auto-read it
- **Zoom ribbon tab:** Zoom is a tool used for viewing your content into a level that is suitable for you
- **Show ribbon tab:** Show ribbon tab consists of ruler for margin measurement, navigation to search words from your content, header & footer to cite or number pages, with other features.

Help tab:

Help is a newly added feature that provides a solution, contact support, and feedback to Microsoft users.

Editing tab:

Editing is also a new feature from Microsoft; this makes you choose to edit your work, review it for additional touch, or view your document

without making any change depending on the users' choice (majorly seen at the top menu of Microsoft Word free web version also in licensed version but not placed above your menu)

CHAPTER THREE
WRESTLING WITH THE TEXT

Manipulating the text

Text manipulation is done in different ways; some of it which are:

Alignment of Text

Text alignment is achieved in four (4) different ways based on an individual purpose of usage:

- **Left Alignment:** By default, all texts are located at your left-hand side; for any reason it is not so, simply click on the arrow indication to return it to your left-hand side or you can highlight it for specialization in a situation where there is more than one line of text. It is also used for heading and footer.

Note: In left alignment, only the left-hand edge will be aligned on the same lines. You can also use *Ctrl + L* as the left alignment shortcut.

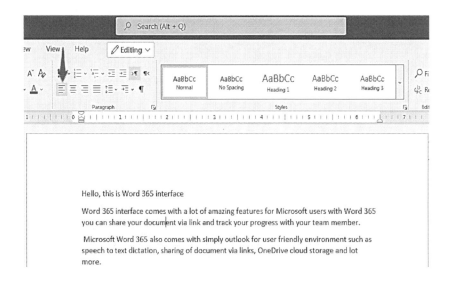

- **Right Alignment:** Right alignment is used majorly for special purposes such as addressing a letter. The arrow in the illustration below indicates the function command responsible for right alignment after you select your text.

Note: In right alignment, only the right-hand edge will be aligned on the same lines. You can also use *Ctrl + R* as the right alignment shortcut

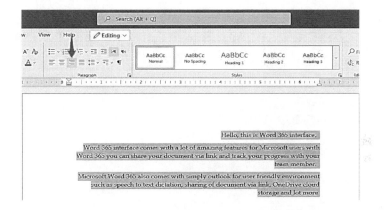

- **Center Alignment:** Center alignment positions your text at the middle of the Word interface; it's majorly used for headings. The pink arrow indicates the command function responsible for center alignment positioning; it is often used for a cover page, quotes, and sometimes headings.

Note: In center alignment, selected text will all be aligned in the middle altogether. You can also use *Ctrl + E* as the center alignment shortcut.

- **Justify Alignment:** Justified text gives your document clean and crisp edges so it looks well organized. Go to the home tab, select the **justify command** as illustrated below.

Note In justify alignment, all selected texts will be justified on the left and right-hand edges altogether. You can also use **Ctrl + J** as the "justify alignment" shortcut.

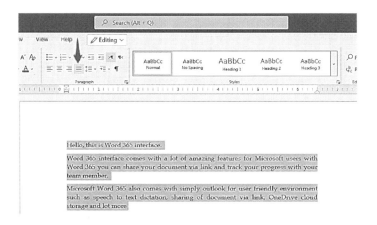

Bolding Text & Adjusting font size

To bold text & adjust the font size by increasing it.

To bold text, select the portion you want to bold, then go to the home tab, select the **B** icon which stands for bold, your text will be in bold format; make sure it is still highlighted then also go to font size as indicated below through the pink arrow, click on it or type the font size you want. You can use **Ctrl + B** as a shortcut to bold text.

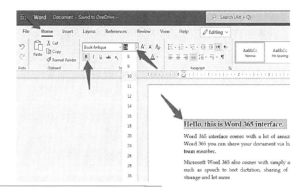

Underlining your text

Go to the home tab

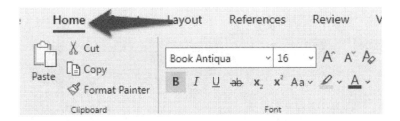

Make sure the text you want to underline is highlighted

Hello, this is Word 365 interface.

Word 365 interface comes with a lot of amazing features for Microsoft users with Word 365 you can share your document via link and track your progress with your team member.

Microsoft Word 365 also comes with simply outlook for user friendly environment such as speech to text dictation, sharing of document via link, OneDrive cloud storage and lot more

Select the **underlined icon (U)**

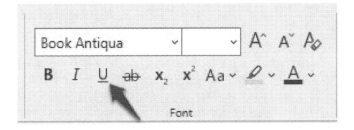

Your highlighted text will become underlined

Word 365 interface comes with a lot of amazing features for Microsoft users with Word 365 you can share your document via link and track your progress with your team member.

Microsoft Word 365 also comes with simply outlook for user friendly environment such as speech to text dictation, sharing of document via link, OneDrive cloud storage and lot more

Italicizing your text

Go to the "home tab", select the text to be italicized by highlighting it with your mouse

Go to the "Font ribbon tab" beside your bold icon (**B**), click on **the italic icon (*I*)**

Then, your highlighted text will become italicized

Hello, this is Word 365 interface.

Word 365 interface comes with a lot of amazing features for Microsoft users with Word 365 you can share your document via link and track your progress with your team member.

Microsoft Word 365 also comes with simply outlook for user friendly environment such as speech to text dictation, sharing of document via link, OneDrive cloud storage and lot more

Selecting Text

You can select text with your mouse by left-clicking and simultaneously dragging through the text you want to select. Your arrow keys can also perform the task by holding the shift key and pressing the arrow key in the direction you want (if it is forward highlighting you want, click on the forward arrow key without leaving your shift key).

Hello, this is Word 365 interf.

Word 365 interface comes with a lot of an
you can share your document via link and

Microsoft Word 365 also comes with sim
speech to text dictation, sharing of docume

Moving & Copying Text

Moving & copying of text, highlight on the text to be moved

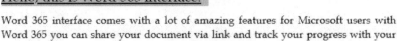

Hello, this is Word 365 interface.

Word 365 interface comes with a lot of amazing features for Microsoft users with Word 365 you can share your document via link and track your progress with your team member.

Microsoft Word 365 also comes with simply outlook for user friendly environment such as speech to text dictation, sharing of document via link, OneDrive cloud storage and lot more.

Left-click and hold, simultaneously drag your mouse on the highlighted text and drag it to anywhere you want it to be. In this illustration, drag beside the last line, then drop it.

Word 365 interface comes with a lot of amazing features for Microsoft users with Word 365 you can share your document via link and track your progress with your team member.

Microsoft Word 365 also comes with simply outlook for user friendly environment such as speech to text dictation, sharing of document via link, OneDrive cloud storage and lot more. Hello, this is Word 365 interface.

Changing the font color of your text

To change the look of your text, highlight your text

Hello, this is Word 365 interface.

If your Word 2019 interface is not on the "home tab" as its default display, simply go to the "home tab" and click on it

Below the "home tab", select "font color" which is identified by a capital letter A underlined with a red stroke as illustrated with an arrow sign below. Are we together? Right let us continue

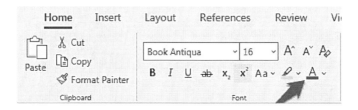

Remember that your text is still selected (highlighted), once you click on "font color", your highlighted text will change to red color.

Hello, this is Word 365 interface.

Choosing more color

You can also click the little arrow beside the "font color" to select your preferred choice, if not found check below for "more colors"

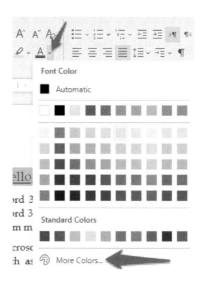

You can also decide to change the *"font style"* known as *"font name"* by selecting *"home tab"*, check on the little arrow beside your current font, dropdown options will be displayed, you can select your preferred choice, but for similarity and understanding purpose select *"Calibri Light (Headings)"*

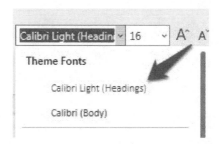

Your highlighted text will take effect immediately

Before

Hello, this is Word 365 interface.

After

Hello, this is Word 365 interface.

Speaking, not Typing Words

Microsoft Word 2019 comes with many added features, one of which is the "Dictate tool" which makes keyboard typing less needed due to time consumption and speaking more needed due to time utilization.

How to use Dictate tools

Go to the *"Home tab"*

At your right-hand side, you will see **"Dictate"**, click on it and two options will appear to you **"Dictate"** & **"Transcribe"**, select **"Dictate"**

Then, you can start your speech to text typing. Make sure you have an internet connection and the illustrated speaker is turned on from a white icon to a red icon

Hello, this is Word 365 interface.

Word 365 interface comes with a lot of amazing features for Microsoft users with Word 365 you can share your document via link and track your progress with your team member.

Microsoft Word 365 also comes with simply outlook for user friendly environment such as speech to text dictation, sharing of document via link, OneDrive cloud storage and lot more.

Applying Text Effects to Texts

- Highlight your text

Hello, this is Word 365 interface.

- In the "Home tab"

- Within your "Font ribbon", you will see "text effects", click on the drop-down arrow

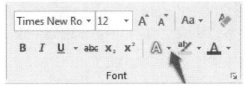

- Select your preferred text effect template and click on it, your text will have the same effect of the format immediately

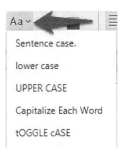

Quick Ways to Handle Case or Capitalization

Change case is a tool for transforming text from small letters to capital letters or a mixture of both with other preferred options. Cases are divided into five (5) segments which are:

- **Sentence case:** Sentence case only capitalizes the first letter of every new paragraph, it is also applicable after a statement ends with a full stop, the next first letter only will be capitalized. To apply sentence case, highlight your text, under the "home tab"

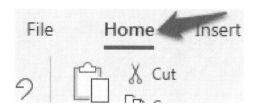

Locate "font ribbon" and select "change case" identified by a capital letter A and a small letter a. Pick "Sentence case"

Then, your text will take effect immediately. Note that every first letter in every paragraph and a new sentence are all in capital letters only, which might affect other words in a statement that should start with a capital letter by default. For example, take a look at the illustration below.

In the first line second paragraph, "Microsoft" carries a small letter 'm' which should always be in capital, not a small letter; that is why it is underlined with a red line, indicating it has a mistake. Right-clicking on the word "Microsoft" will give you the right spelling.

Hello, this is word 365 interface.

Word 365 interface comes with a lot of amazing features for microsoft users with word 365 you can share your document via link and track your progress with your team member. I am a new sentence after a full stop

Microsoft word 365 also comes with simply outlook for user friendly environment such as speech to text dictation, sharing of document via link, onedrive cloud storage and lot more.

- **Lower case:** Lower case makes every word be in a small letter. To apply lower case, highlight the portion you want to effect lower case into, for this illustration, let's highlight all the text

Hello, this is word 365 interface.

Word 365 interface comes with a lot of amazing features for Microsoft users with word 365 you can share your document via link and track your progress with your team member. I am a new sentence after a full stop

Microsoft word 365 also comes with simply outlook for user friendly environment such as speech to text dictation, sharing of document via link, onedrive cloud storage and lot more.

Go to the "Home tab"

Locate "font ribbon" and select "change case". Pick "lower case"

Then, it will take effect immediately on your text. Note that all the text including the first letter of every paragraph will reflect lower case by default

hello, this is word 365 interface.

word 365 interface comes with a lot of amazing features for microsoft users with word 365 you can share your document via link and track your progress with your team member. i am a new sentence after a full stop

microsoft word 365 also comes with simply outlook for user friendly environment such as speech to text dictation, sharing of document via link, onedrive cloud storage and lot more.

- **Upper case:** Upper case is used to capitalize words. This is majorly used for headings or a title that reflect what a bunch of words represent. To apply upper case, kindly highlight your text

hello, this is word 365 interface.

word 365 interface comes with a lot of amazing features for microsoft users with word 365 you can share your document via link and track your progress with your team member. i am a new sentence after a full stop

microsoft word 365 also comes with simply outlook for user friendly environment such as speech to text dictation, sharing of document via link, onedrive cloud storage and lot more.

Go to the "Home tab"

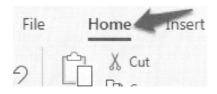

Locate "font ribbon" and select "change case". Pick "upper case"

Then, it will take effect on your text immediately. Note all text will be capitalized by default

HELLO, THIS IS WORD 365 INTERFACE.

WORD 365 INTERFACE COMES WITH A LOT OF AMAZING FEATURES FOR MICROSOFT USERS WITH WORD 365 YOU CAN SHARE YOUR DOCUMENT VIA LINK AND TRACK YOUR PROGRESS WITH YOUR TEAM MEMBER. I AM A NEW SENTENCE AFTER A FULL STOP

MICROSOFT WORD 365 ALSO COMES WITH SIMPLY OUTLOOK FOR USER FRIENDLY ENVIRONMENT SUCH AS SPEECH TO TEXT DICTATION, SHARING OF DOCUMENT VIA LINK, ONEDRIVE CLOUD STORAGE AND LOT MORE.

- **Capitalize each word:** this is used to capitalize each word in a sentence. To apply this, highlight all your text or the specific one you want it to affect; based on this guide we will be highlighting all, after highlighting all

Hello, this is word 365 interface.

Word 365 interface comes with a lot of amazing features for Microsoft users with word 365 you can share your document via link and track your progress with your team member. I am a new sentence after a full stop

Microsoft word 365 also comes with simply outlook for user friendly environment such as speech to text dictation, sharing of document via link, onedrive cloud storage and lot more.

Go to the "Home tab"

Locate "font ribbon" and select "change case", pick "Capitalize each word"

Then, it will take effect immediately on your text. Note all first words will be capitalized by default.

Hello, This Is Word 365 Interface.

Word 365 Interface Comes With A Lot Of Amazing Features For Microsoft Users With Word 365 You Can Share Your Document Via Link And Track Your Progress With Your Team Member. I Am A New Sentence After A Full Stop

Microsoft Word 365 Also Comes With Simply Outlook For User Friendly Environment Such As Speech To Text Dictation, Sharing Of Document Via Link, Onedrive Cloud Storage And Lot More.

- **Toggle word:** Toggle word is the opposite of "capitalize each word". In the toggle word, every first letter of a paragraph or a letter of a new sentence is in small letters while others are in capital letters. To apply toggle word, simply highlight all your text as usual

> Hello, this is word 365 interface.
>
> Word 365 interface comes with a lot of amazing features for Microsoft users with word 365 you can share your document via link and track your progress with your team member. I am a new sentence after a full stop
>
> Microsoft word 365 also comes with simply outlook for user friendly environment such as speech to text dictation, sharing of document via link, onedrive cloud storage and lot more.

Go to the "Home tab"

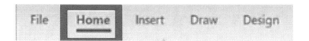

Locate "font ribbon" and select "change case". Pick "toggle case"

Then, it will take effect immediately on your text. Note that all first letters in each paragraph and a new text after a full stop will start with a small letter.

> hELLO, THIS IS WORD 365 INTERFACE.
>
> wORD 365 INTERFACE COMES WITH A LOT OF AMAZING FEATURES FOR mICROSOFT USERS WITH WORD 365 YOU CAN SHARE YOUR DOCUMENT VIA LINK AND TRACK YOUR PROGRESS WITH YOUR TEAM MEMBER. i AM A NEW SENTENCE AFTER A FULL STOP
>
> mICROSOFT WORD 365 ALSO COMES WITH SIMPLY OUTLOOK FOR USER FRIENDLY ENVIRONMENT SUCH AS SPEECH TO TEXT DICTATION, SHARING OF DOCUMENT VIA LINK, ONEDRIVE CLOUD STORAGE AND LOT MORE.

Entering Symbols and Foreign Characters

Symbol as its name implies is a sign or a tag used to list and categorize text. Symbols include a variety of options such as mathematical symbols, currency symbols, copyright symbols, and lots more.

- How to apply it; assuming we want to create a fruit list and the first fruit on the list is orange, point your cursor to where orange is located at the beginning of the letter "O" of orange.

List of fruits

Orange

Apple

Dragon Fruit

Blueberries

Melon

Raspberries

- Now, go to the "Insert" menu" bar

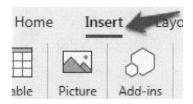

- You will locate your "symbols ribbon" at your right-hand side

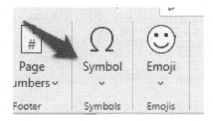

- Click on "Symbol's ribbon" to select your preferred choice

- Once selected, it will affect the cursor position, you can do the same to other items on the list

List of fruits

• Orange

Apple

Dragon Fruit

Blueberries

Melon

Raspberries

Creating Hyperlinks

Creating a hyperlink is a great feature of Microsoft Word that redirects you to the web for more info on the linked text. It is majorly used for references.

Linking a hyperlink to a web page

- First, select your text to be linked

Hello, this is word 365 interface.

- Secondly, go to "Insert menu bar"

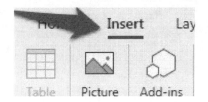

- By your right-hand side, you will see "link", click on it

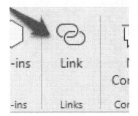

- Once you click on it, a dialog box will appear (still make sure your link text is highlighted), if your text is still highlighted, it will show automatically on the **"Display text box".** Let us assume we want our link to redirect us into Microsoft website, simply type the website, www.microsoft.com and click the **"Insert option".** This is your result for Microsoft Word 2019 web users.

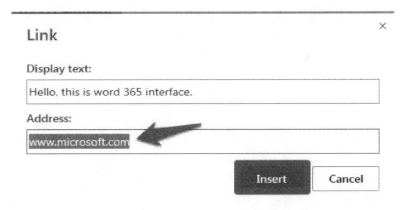

For Microsoft Word 2019 license users, this is your result, locate **"Existing file or web page"** by your left-hand side which is titled **"Link to",** select the first option **"Current folder"** under **"Look in",** once selected, look down, you will see another titled bar named **"Address"** enter your redirected address and press **"Ok".**

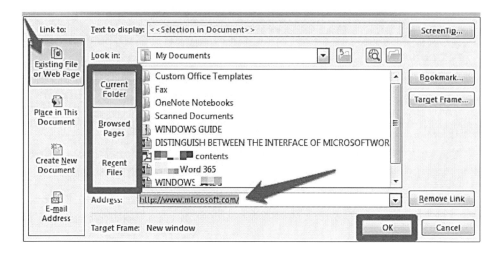

- Your highlighted text will be converted into a blue color with an underline

<u>Hello, this is word 365 interface.</u>

- To redirect into the Microsoft link, kindly press your "Ctrl key + Left-click". You will be redirected to the Microsoft website we inputted

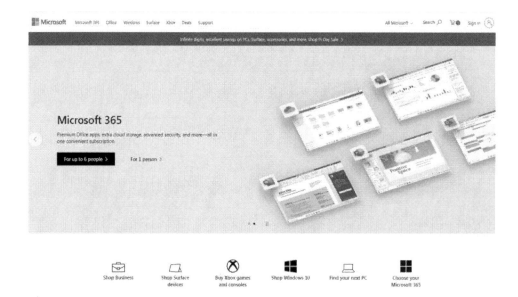

Note: this can be used on any other website of your choice.

Creating a hyperlink to another place in your file.

Note: By now, this feature of linking one file to another has not yet been included on Microsoft Word 2019 Cloud version, it's still under improvement, and due to being a free version, some features are withdrawn and only available on Microsoft Word 2019 installed application version which comes with a licensed product key that can be purchased from Microsoft official website (www.microsoft.com). So, this illustration is based on Microsoft Word 2019 licensed version. Are we together? Alright, can we continue? Okay.

- Select the text you want to link into another file

Hello, this is word 365 interface.

- Go to **"Insert"** in the menu bar

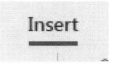

- By your right-hand side, locate the **"Link ribbon"** click on it

- A dialog box will pop up, select **"Existing file or web page"**, then click on **"Current folder"** or **"Browsed pages"** to locate your file, once seen, select it as illustrated in arrow three, it will be automatically selected in the "Address bar". Above is our highlighted text named **"text to display"**, except you highlight it as explained above, it won't reflect on the above dialog box. Click "ok" to see the effect.

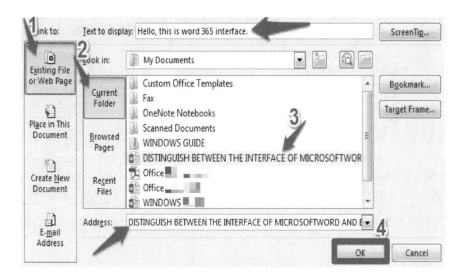

- Below must be your outcome, the highlighted text will change from its normal black color to blue or orange color, press Ctrl and simultaneously left-click on your mouse.

Hello, this is word 365 interface.

- A dialog box will be displayed warning you that hyperlinks might be harmful to your computer and data, that you should only click those hyperlinks you trusted such as the one you created yourself and other trusted ones. Click *"Yes"* to proceed

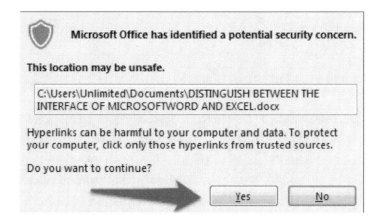

- Your linked file will be opened automatically

Word Handles Text Better

Word is made for text documents, including letters, books and academic papers. Text in Excel is usually a brief snippet used to describe the meaning of a number.

Word's for Printing

A Word document is formatted to fit on a specific size page with the text automatically flowing from one page to the next. Excel supports printing, but its page breaks are not obvious, and because it's printing area can extend multiple pages horizontally as well as vertically the page breaks can be difficult to manage.

Creating an email hyperlink

- Select the text you want to link into another file

Hello, this is word 365 interface.

- Go to "Insert menu bar"

- By your right-hand side, locate **"Link ribbon",** click on it

- Link ribbon dialog box will pop up with multiple options, for this session we are going to create an email link. Don't let us forget our highlighted text at the top side that will still reflect itself as a means of reminding us that we highlighted a text before starting this process of creating an email link which is **"Hello, this is Word 2019 interface."**

Below at your left-hand side is your "Email Address", click on it, you will be brought here, enter your **"Email address"** & **"Subject"** and **"Recently used email address"** (This is optional except you have been using email linking before all your previous activities will be displayed here). Once you are done filling, click "Ok"

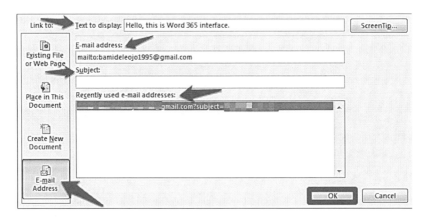

- Your highlighted text will automatically change from black to either blue or orange color as a sign that our process of creating a link via email is successful. To confirm, press Ctrl and simultaneously left-click, your cursor arrow pointer will change to the hand-click icon, then left-click to redirect you to your inserted details.

Hello, this is word 365 interface.

Removing hyperlink

No effect without remedy, every action on Microsoft Word has a way of maneuvering it. To remove the hyperlink on your affected text.

- Select your affected text that has a hyperlink effect

Hello, this is Word 365 interface.

- Go to "Insert menu bar"

Insert

- By your right-hand side, locate *"Link ribbon"* click on it

Link

- The Link dialog box will appear, at your right-hand side as illustrated with the arrow below, click on *"Remove Link"* and hit *"Ok"*

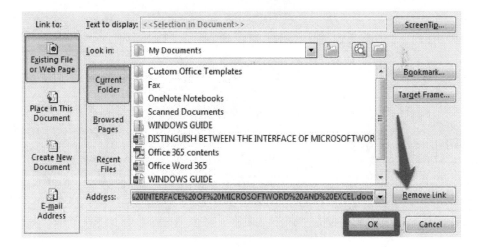

- Your highlighted linked text will automatically be removed from the hyperlink and it will become normal text with your default black color.

Hello, this is word 365 interface.

Notification

Notification gives more awareness about a newly added feature, which is one of the reasons software companies are all gradually moving online to reduce upgrading and different release.

How to rename your document

- Simply click on **"File"**

A dialog box will slide in by your left-hand side, look for **"save as"**, click on it

Note that there is no save button on Word 2019 free online version, it AutoSaves itself online. Once you select **"Save as"**, a slide will appear beside the blue 'Save as' slide at your right, look for **"Rename"** and click on it.

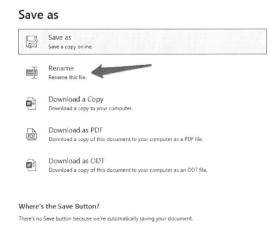

A dialog box will appear titled **"File Name"**, you can rename your document as you wish

How to Save a document directly to your PC

- Go to "File menu"

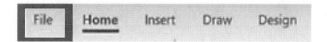

- Select "Save option"

- A dialog box will appear, select the location you want to save, name your document on the "File name box" and click "Save".

Note: saving your document on your PC is only for licensed users, Microsoft Word online free version saves automatically online on OneDrive storage.

How to Save a document directly to your OneDrive cloud storage?

- Go to "file menu"

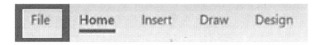

- You will see multiple options, select "Save as"

- A dialog box will appear, you will see the "OneDrive" option, once you click it, your document will be saved online. If you have many folders on your OneDrive storage, you will be asked to choose the destination you want your work to be saved in, once done, hit "Save".

Where does my document go to?

Your document majorly comes to your PC storage or OneDrive cloud storage. OneDrive cloud storage serves as a physical hard disk drive, while PC storage is your system hard disk storage. When you put your files and photos in OneDrive, they are always at your fingertip, no matter where you are. It is important to note that your files are private until you decide to collaborate by sharing your documents with your team and edit together in real-time by sending them a link and authorization access to edit.

How to upgrade your Microsoft 2019 web free version

Upgrading is only recommended for office usage or personal usage that has more files than the normal 1 Gigabyte free storage capacity can contain in the long run. Once you are among the license subscribers, you will be informed depending on your plan.

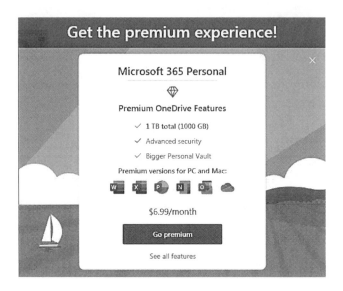

It is advisable to know what you want to achieve with an upgrade in order not to be charged unnecessarily.

CHAPTER FOUR

SPEED TECHNIQUES WORTH KNOWING ABOUT

Undoing and Redoing Commands

Undoing and repeating commands are more of erasing and recalling words

To Undo Text

- After typing a bunch of text on Word 2019

> Hello, this is word 365 interface.
>
> Word 365 interface comes with a lot of amazing features for Microsoft users with word 365 you can share your document via link and track your progress with your team member.

- You can press Ctrl + Z to undo your text, it will gradually backward your text

> Hello, this is word 365 interface.
>
> Word 365 interface comes with a lot of amazing features for Microsoft users with word 365 you can share your document via link

- Or you highlight the part to be removed and press **"backspace"** from your keyboard to remove it.

> Hello, this is word 365 interface.
>
> Word 365 interface comes with a lot of amazing features for Microsoft users with word 365 you can share your document via link and track your progress with your team member.

- You can also use Word 2019 undo icon to backward your text, either way, your text will be undone. Simply go to the **"home tab",** which is your default display interface and by your left-hand side you will see your Undo icon. The first arrow is your undo icon facing backward while the second one is your redo icon facing forward.

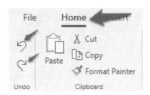

To Redo Text

- After typing a bunch of text on Word 2019

    Hello, this is word 365 interface.

    Word 365 interface comes with a lot of amazing features for Microsoft users with word 365 you
    can share your document via link and track your progress with your team member|

- You can press Ctrl + Y to redo your text, it will redo what you earlier undo

    Hello, this is word 365 interface.

    Word 365 interface comes with a lot of amazing features for Microsoft users with word 365 you
    can share your document via link|

- You can also use Word 2019 redo icon to forward your text only if it had been earlier back-warded. Your text will redo when you mistakenly remove or delete some text. To use the redo icon, simply go to the **"home tab"** which is your default display interface, by your left-hand side, you will see your redo icon the first arrow is your undo facing backward while the second one is your redo facing forward.

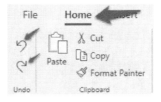

Zooming In and Zooming Out

Zooming In & Zooming Out is a feature of Microsoft Word that makes the Word interface clearer and more readable depending on the user's choice. You see that Microsoft Word is embedded with simplicity and flexibility.

How to Zoom In & Zoom Out

- Go to *"View menu bar"*

- Under *"View menu bar",* select *"Zoom percentage"*

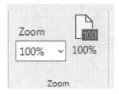

- Once you click on the little arrow beside the *"100%"*, dropdown options of Zooming In & Zooming Out will pop up, select your preferred choice and it will affect the entire interface of your current working document.

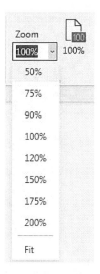

- The other *"100%",* will return your zooming in & out to 100% default displayed zooming settings

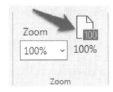

Viewing a File through More than One Window

Viewing of file through more than one Window creates the possibility to work in another Window and not affect your original Window.

Steps on how to apply it

- From your current opened document, go to "View menu bar" by your right-hand side

- It is advisable to purchase a license Microsoft Office installation software because the one online is still very much under progressive development; not all features are on Word 2019 web base.

- Under the "view menu bar", click on "New Window" (which is known as document interface), your current document which is opened will be duplicated and named "document:1" by default, except you rename it. Another duplicated one will be named "document:2"

- Any changes in one will automatically lead to the same changes in the other.

Correcting Typos

Errors can be an omission in typing and as long as a human being is concerned, a computer can never use itself, but rather, human determines the behavior of a PC, this is the reason for misspelling and other mistakes made by PC users. Yet, Microsoft researcher team members look for a remedy to this issue, which leads to auto-correct in Microsoft packages.

Steps on how to enable auto-correct

Automatically, auto-correct is always activated on all Microsoft packages. Due to one reason or the other, if it is not, simply follow this simple process:

- Go to "Review menu bar"

- At your left-hand side on "Proofing ribbon", click on "Spelling & Grammar"

- Once you click on "Spelling & Grammar", auto-correct for error detection are shown one at a time as they occur in your document. You must deal with them one after the other (serially).

Entering Text Quickly with the Auto-Correct

Entering text quickly with the auto-correct command is often used for frequently used words such as an address, greetings text format, letter text template, and other text purposes.

Steps on how to go about AutoCorrect Command

- First, select the text you do use often by highlighting it

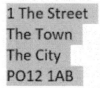

- Go to *"Insert menu bar"*

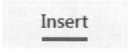

- By your right-hand side, you will see "Quick Parts", click on it and select *"Save Selection to Quick Part Gallery"*

- Make sure your selected text is still highlighted, if not *"Save Selection to Quick Part Gallery"* will not be visible

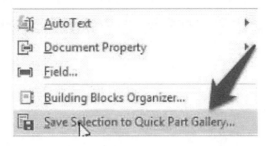

- After you select "Save Selection to Quick Part Gallery", a dialog box will appear with the name "Create New Building Block", there, you can rename the title of the highlighted text, and in the "Gallery" text box, select "Quick Part"

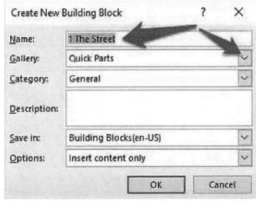

- Make sure this is what you inputted, if you followed and typed the highlighted text as instructed, for understanding purpose, leave the "Description", "Save in" & "Options" the way it is. Once done, press "Ok"

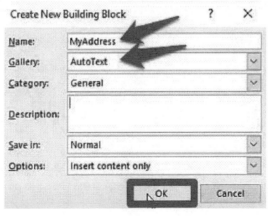

How do you assign a shortcut key to bring forth your auto text entry?

- Go to your "file menu bar" which is also known as "file menu"

- Under "file menu", select "Options"

- A dialog box will appear on your left-hand side, select "Customize Ribbon"

- By your right-hand side, "Customize Ribbon" features will appear, below it, you will see "Keyboard shortcuts", click on "Customize"

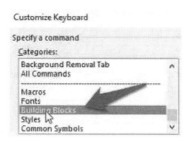

- Another dialog box will appear titled "Categories", search for "Building Blocks"

- Once you have located "Building Blocks", click on it, building blocks features will appear beside it at your right-hand side, locate "MyAddress"; based on my illustration on "Steps on how to go about AutoCorrect Command", I renamed the "Name" text box under "Create New Building Block" as "MyAddress" that is why I can locate it here. In case you name yours differently, search for it, or else, go back and follow how I did mine.

- Once selected, below it is a dialog box where you can assign a shortcut key to it, it is titled "Press new shortcut keys:"

- I will be inserting my preferred shortcut command which is "Ctrl+Shift+M". I will advise you do the same in order not to make any mistake, once you understand it you can repeat the process yourself.

- Once done, look at your left-hand side and click on "Assign"

- Above the "Assign" option, your shortcut command will appear on a box titled "Current keys:" as against the previous title- "Press new shortcut keys:"

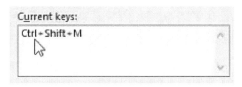

- Then, click on "Close"

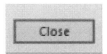

- Also, click on "Ok" on the "Customize the Ribbon and keyboard shortcuts" dialog box that leads to "Keyboard shortcuts"

- Now delete your highlighted text or open a new document to confirm our newly added auto text shortcut key.

- Once you press "Ctrl + Shift + M" from your keyboard, your auto-text will reappear back automatically.

Tips

Practice makes perfect, try doing something different by changing the address and shortcut to suit your taste and run your newly added shortcut to see if you will get it correctly without following my exact text & shortcut.

CHAPTER FIVE
LAYING OUT TEXT AND PAGES

Paragraphs and Formatting

It is important to note that paragraphs in a document cannot be ignored as far as typing is concerned. A Paragraph has different clicking methods: Single-click, double-click, triple-click, and click and drag

- *Single-Click:* Single-clicking on a paragraph only makes the cursor point on a particular text in the paragraph.

> *Single-Click* single clicking
> cursor point on a particular

- *Double-Click:* Double-clicking in a paragraph highlights a particular text

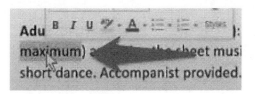

- *Triple-Click:* Triple-clicking highlights the whole text in a paragraph as illustrated below

> It is important to note that paragraph in a document cannot be ignored as far as typing is concerned. Paragraph has different clicking methods: Single click, double click, triple click and click and drag

- *Click and Drag:* Click and drag selects within or beyond a paragraph depending on the user's preference.

Adult singers (18 years and older): Please prepare an upbeat song (other than one from the show) and bring the sheet music with you.

Adult dancers (18 years and older): Please prepare a short dance (2 minutes maximum) and bring the sheet music with you. Tap dancing is encouraged for the short dance. Accompanist provided.

Youth singers and dancers (9 to 14 years): You do not need to prepare a song.

Paragraph Settings

Paragraph Settings help to finetune the layout of the current paragraph, including spacing, indentation, alignment, outline level with other features.

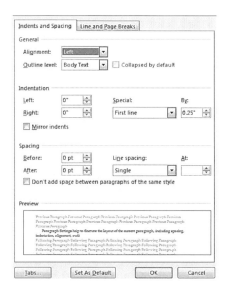

Page Formatting & Cover page

Page formatting is a tool that determines the outlook of your pages such as page margins, page orientation, page size, page columns, and lots more.

- **Page Margins:** Page margin is used to set the sizes for the entire document or the current section. Page Margins gives the privilege to choose from several commonly used margin formats or customize your own. Anyone you select will automatically affect your current working document.

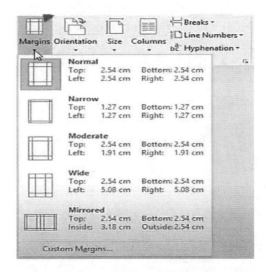

- **Page Orientation:** Page orientation determines the outlook of your page in portrait or landscape format. Anyone you select will automatically affect your current document.

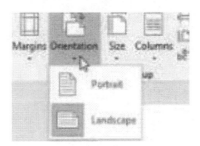

Page Size: Page size comes in various forms but by default, A4 is the standard page size from Microsoft

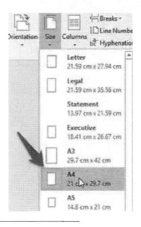

Page Columns: Page columns give you the privilege to slit your text into two or more columns. You can also choose the width and spacing of your columns, or use one of the preset formats

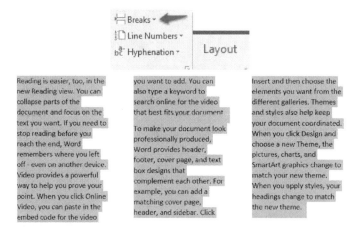

Above is an example of three columns, all you need to do is to highlight the area you want to make changes to, if you don't select it, the whole of your pages will be affected by the columns you choose.

Setting Up and Changing the Margins

Note: By default, Word document comes with default configurations, one of which is the normal margin.

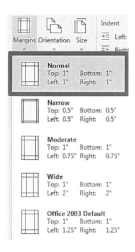

How to change your margins

- Go to "Layout tab"

- By your left-hand side, you will see "Margins"

- Once you click in, your default "Margin" settings will be on "Normal".

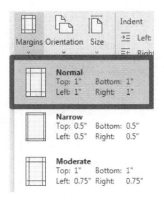

- Scroll through to select other desired options which will automatically affect your active opened document.

Note: Adjusting or changing of margin only affects your opened document, and it remains when you save the effect. For web users, you don't need to save, it automatically saves into your OneDrive cloud storage, while for offline users go to "file menu", and then you will see the save option. OneDrive storage is also available for offline users as long as you are connected to your Microsoft account.

Inserting a Section Break for Formatting Purposes

Before illustrating how to insert a section break format, it is important to know what "section break" is all about. Section break gives a separation between texts and sends the separated one into another page

- Point your cursor to where you want to set a section break

  Video provides a powerful way to help you prove your point. When you click Online Video, you can paste in the embed code for the video you want to add. You can also type a keyword to search online for the video that best fits your document. To make your document look professionally produced, Word provides header, footer, cover page, and text box designs that complement each other. For example, you can add a matching cover page, header, and sidebar. Click Insert and then choose the elements you want from the different galleries.

  Themes and styles also help keep your document coordinated. When you click Design and choose a new Theme, the pictures, charts, and SmartArt graphics change to match your new theme. When you apply

- Go to the "Layout tab"

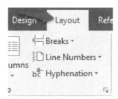

- Select "Breaks"

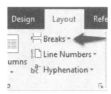

- Then, you can select "Page" to make your text have the section break effect

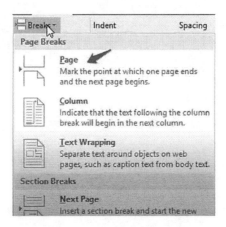

- Once you select "Page", the text where your cursor pointer is located will be automatically separated into a new page

Video provides a powerful way to help you prove your point. When you click Online Video, you can paste in the embed code for the video you want to add. You can also type a keyword to search online for the video that best fits your document. To make your document look professionally produced, Word provides header, footer, cover page, and text box designs that complement each other.

For example, you can add a matching cover page, header, and sidebar. Click Insert and then choose the elements you want from the different galleries.

Themes and styles also help keep your document coordinated. When you click Design and choose a new Theme, the pictures, charts, and SmartArt graphics change to match your new theme. When you apply styles, your headings change to match the new theme. Save time in Word with new buttons that show up where you need them. To change the way a picture fits in your document, click it and a button for layout options appears next to it. When you work on a table, click where you want to add a row or a column, and then click the plus sign.

There is also a shortcut to section break, once you set your cursor to the location you want to part, simply hold down your "Ctrl key" and hit "Enter key" from your keyboard. The point where your cursor is will automatically be parted into another page.

Cover Page

A Cover Page is a front guide of every documentation, project, brochure, and other documents which gives a summarization of what your content entails.

How to Insert a Cover Page on your Document

- Go to "Insert tab"

- At your left-hand side, you will see *"Cover Page"*

- Click in to see multiple built-in "Cover Page" templates, select your preferred choice

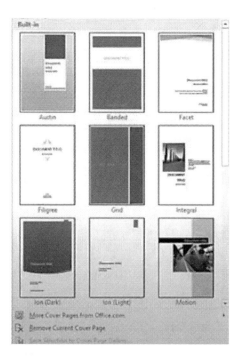

- Once you select your preferred choice, your selected cover page will occupy your front page

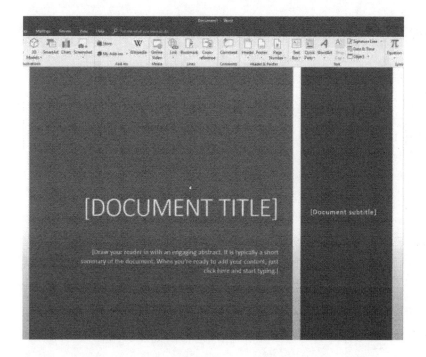

- Then, you can start editing the title page, the writeup below your title, subtitle, and other aspects depending on the template you selected

Indenting Paragraphs

- Go to the "Home tab" which is your default Word 2019 interface

- At your right-hand side, locate the "Paragraph ribbon", you will see the decrease & increase indent

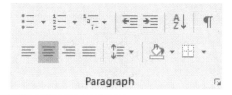

What is Decrease & Increase Indent?

Decrease Indent: Decrease indent moves your paragraph closer to your margin

Increase Indent: Increase indent moves your paragraph farther from your margin

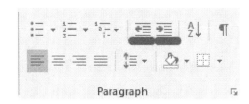

Paragraph

- Once you select increase indent, your paragraph moves to your right-hand side

  ⊿ Word Handles Text Better

  Word is made for text documents, includir
  Excel is usually a brief snippet used to desc

- And if you select decrease indent, your paragraph will move back to your left-hand side

  ⁴ Word Handles Text Better

  Word is made for text documents, including
  usually a brief snippet used to describe the n

- Decrease indent & Increase indent are both used depending on what is required or what the user wants to achieve

Numbering the Pages

Page Numbering is a way of making your content arranged serially for orderliness and reference purposes.

How to Insert Page Numbering

- Go to "Insert tab"

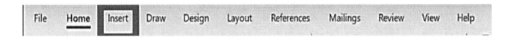

- At your right-hand side, you will see "Page Number" under "Header & Footer ribbon"

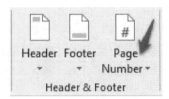

- Click on "Page Number", once you click on it, you will be given multiple options on where you want your page numbering to be positioned such as "Top of Page", "Bottom of Page", "Page Margins", "Current Position".

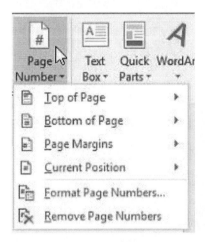

Or you can decide how you want your page numbering to look by clicking on "Format Page Numbers". A dialog box will appear for you to configure your Page Numberings such as "Number format", where you want to start effecting from, and lots more. Once you fill it, press "ok" to effect changes

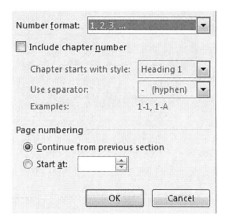

- Assuming you want the "Bottom of Page" option, click on "Bottom of Page" which is the normally used page numbering
- A dialog box will appear beside it, choose the middle numbering format

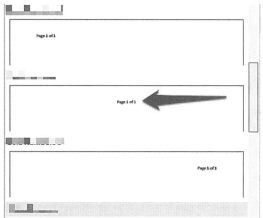

- By default, all your text will automatically be numbered serially

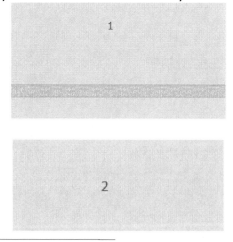

Remove Page Numbering

- Go to "Insert tab"

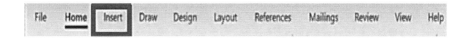

- At your right-hand side, you will see "Page Number" under "Header & Footer ribbon"

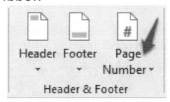

- Click on "Page Number", once you click on it, you will be given multiple options, look for "Remove Page Numbers", click on it, and every page numbering on your current opened document will be removed automatically

Putting Header on Pages

- Go to "Insert tab"

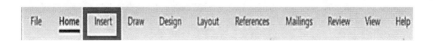

- At your right-hand side, look for "Header"

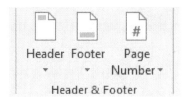

- A dialog box will appear, select your preferred alignment positioning

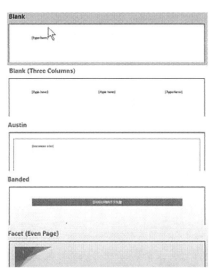

- Once done, you will be brought to your header editing edge to input your text

DISTINGUISH BETWEEN THE AND EXCEL

Word Handles Text Better

Note: You can also double-click on the top empty edge of your document to make use of the header format.

Removing Header from Pages

- Go to "Insert tab"

- At your right-hand side, locate "Header" and click on it

- A dialog box will appear below "Header" showing you header positioning, look down the list you will see "Remove Header". Once you click on it, your "Header" will be removed automatically

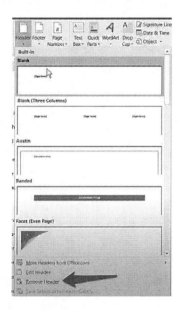

Putting Footer on Pages

- Go to "Insert tab"

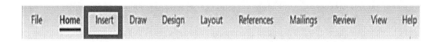

- At your right-hand side, locate "Footer" and click on it

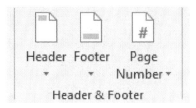

- A dialog box will appear, select your preferred alignment positioning

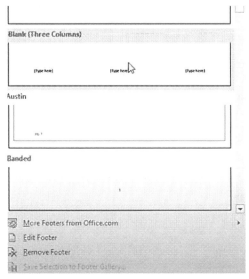

- Once done, you will be brought to your footer editing edge to input your text

Note: You can also double-click below the page you want to insert the footer, you will be brought to an empty or footer format area where you can input your footer format.

Removing Footer from Pages

- Go to "Insert tab"

- At your right-hand side, locate "Header", click on it

- A dialog box will appear below "Footer" showing you footer positioning, look down the list, you will see "Remove Footer". Once you click on it, your "Footer" will be removed automatically

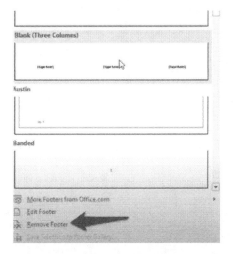

Line and Paragraph Spacing

Line and Paragraph determine how much space will be allocated between lines of text or between paragraphs. To apply the same spacing to your whole document, use the Paragraph spacing options on the "Design tab".

Adjusting the space between lines

- Go to "Home tab" which is Word 2019 default displayed interface

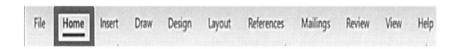

- At your right-hand side, locate "Paragraph ribbon", you will see the "line and paragraph spacing" icon

Paragraph

- Once you click in, you will be shown multiple options for line spacing between text or if your preferred choice is not in the list, click on "Line Spacing Options" to manually decide your choice

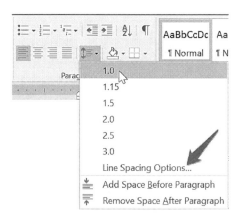

- If you click "Line Spacing Options", a dialog box will appear for you to decide your line spacing measurement "Before" & "After" once set to your preferred choice, hit the "Ok" button below

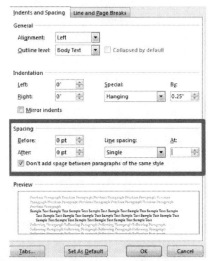

- It will automatically take effect on your opened document.

Adjusting the space between paragraphs

- Go to the "Design tab"

- Look at your right-hand side and select "Paragraph Spacing"

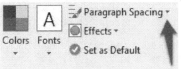

- A dialog box will appear displaying multiple options available for use

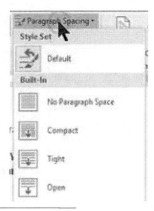

- Once you select your preferred choice, the effect will take place automatically on the entire document.

The difference between line spacing under "home tab" & paragraph spacing under "design tab"

Line and paragraph spacing under *"home tab"* adjust text manually, and it is done per paragraph, except you highlight the whole of your document.

Paragraph spacing under the *"design tab"* adjusts text automatically. This affects the whole of your document.

Creating Numbered and Bulleted Lists

Creating Bulleted Lists

- Highlight the portion of text that you want bullet list to take an effect on

- Go to the "Home tab" which is your display settings interface

- At your left-hand side in the "Paragraph ribbon", the first tool you will see is the "Bullets list".

- In the "Bullet" list, select your preferred choice from your "bullet library" and click on it

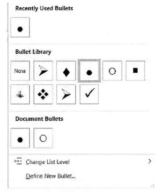

- It will automatically take an effect on your highlighted text

- Or you can click on "bullet list" and select your preferred choice on a free space in the document which also grants you access to be listing your item automatically.

- Once you enter an item and you click on "Enter key" from your keyboard, it will continue the bulleting automatically

Creating Numbered Lists

- Highlight the portion of text that you want the numbering list to affect

List of fruits
Orange
Apple
Blueberry
Watermelon
Guava
Banana

- Go to the "Home tab" which is your display settings interface

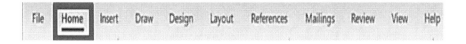

- On your left-hand side, locate the "Paragraph ribbon", the second tool you will see beside the bullet's icon is the "numbering list", click on it.

- You will be given many options to pick from, you can pick the numbering of your choice.

Note: The numbering library consists of number listing, alphabet listing, and roman figure listing, it's not designed for numbers alone.

- Immediately you select the number list (you can pick your preferred choice), it will automatically take effect on your highlighted text.

List of fruits

1. Orange
2. Apple
3. Blueberry
4. Watermelon
5. Guava
6. Banana

- Or you can check "number list" and select your preferred choice on a free space in your document which also grants you access to be listing your item automatically.

List of fruits

1. |

- Once you enter an item and you click your "Enter key" from your keyboard it will automatically continue the numbering.

List of fruits

1. Orange
2. |

Constructing lists of your own

Either bullets list or numbering list, you can construct your own preferred choice of bullets list or numbering list

For bullets list

- Go to the "home tab" which is your default displayed interface

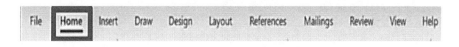

- At your right-hand side, you will see the "Paragraph ribbon", select bullets list

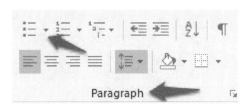

- Select "Define New Bullet"

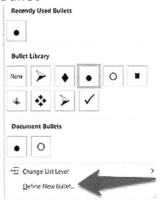

- A dialog box will appear titled "Bullet character" which comes with design tools for your configuration bullet list, you can make your list as an image format by browsing through your PC to select your preferred image, or mathematical symbols and also set the alignment positioning. Once done with the settings, hit the "Ok" option.

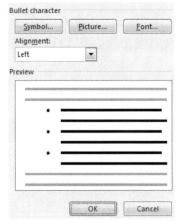

- Your selected image and other adjusted styles will take effect by default

List of fruits
- Orange
- Apple
- Blueberry
- Watermelon
- Guava
- Banana

For numbering list

- Go to the "home tab" which is your default displayed interface

- Around the middle area, you will see the "Paragraph ribbon", select the numbering list

- Select "Define New Number Format"

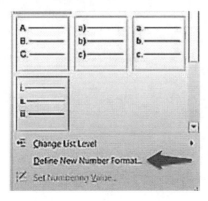

- A dialog box will appear titled "Number format", on the numbering list, you can't add an image or symbol, but you can determine your numbering format, be it alphabet format, roman figure format, or numbering format

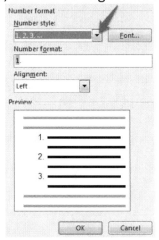

- Since the default numbering is numeric, let's choose the Roman figure to see the effect in a different way

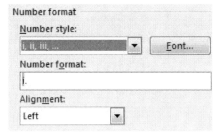

- Once selected, click "Ok"

- By default, the selected roman figure will take effect immediately.

Note: There are other numbering formats available; you can choose something different after trying what we just accomplished.

List of fruits
    i.   Orange
    ii.   Apple
    iii.   Blueberry
    iv.   Watermelon
    v.   Guava
    vi.   Banana

Managing a multilevel list

- Highlight the portion of text that you want numbering list or bullet list to affect

List of fruits
Orange
Apple
Blueberry
Mango
Watermelon
Pineapple
Guava
Banana

- Go to the "Home tab" which is your display settings interface

- At your right-hand side in the paragraph ribbon, you will see "multilevel list", as indicated below with a pink straight line

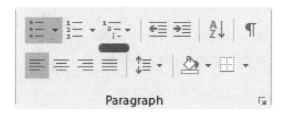

Paragraph

- Once you click on "Multilevel List", a dropdown of multilevel list options will appear

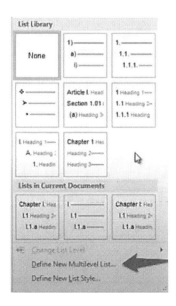

- Select "Define New Multilevel List" as illustrated above and a dialog box will appear named "Click level to modify", you will be instructed to set your multilevel list to your preferred taste.

  The first numbering at your left is the first list item, the second is the second item till numbering 9 for the ninth item. Below is the "Enter formatting for number" option where you edit the dropdown (sub-list) item. Once done, click "ok".

- Now back to our highlighted items

List of fruits
Orange
Apple
Blueberry
Mango
Watermelon
Pineapple
Guava
Banana

- Let make use of the "Numbering list"

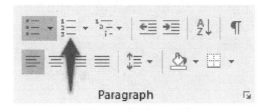

Paragraph

- Select numeric list, double-click on it

- Once it has been numbered, this will be the outcome of your highlighted items, but this is not what we still want to achieve

---

List of fruits
1. Orange
2. Apple
3. Blueberry
4. Mango
5. Watermelon
6. Pineapple
7. Guava
8. Banana

- Now, highlight only "Apple", "Blueberry", "Mango", "Watermelon", "Pineapple" (item 2 to 6 on the list).

List of fruits
1. Orange
2. Apple
3. Blueberry
4. Mango
5. Watermelon
6. Pineapple
7. Guava
8. Banana

- Then, press the "Tab" key on your keyboard located by your left-hand side, you will get this result; "orange" will have a sub-list below itself. We are getting closer but we can do beyond this, let's continue

List of fruits
1. Orange
   a. Apple
   b. Blueberry
   c. Mango
   d. Watermelon
   e. Pineapple
2. Guava
3. Banana

- Now, highlight only "Blueberry" & "Mango"

List of fruits
1. Orange
   a. Apple
   b. Blueberry
   c. Mango
   d. Watermelon
   e. Pineapple
2. Guava
3. Banana

- Then, press your "Tab" key located on your keyboard by your left-hand side, by default "Apple" will have a sub-list of items which are "Blueberry" & "Mango"

List of fruits
1. Orange
   a. Apple
      i. Blueberry
      ii. Mango
   b. Watermelon
   c. Pineapple
2. Guava
3. Banana

You can also play around it to achieve something different from my illustration. Now, you see how flexible working on Word 2019 is.

Working with Tabs

Tab on your keyboard has been a wonderfully used key function, the beauty of it is that it can also be set to suit you.

- Go to your "Home tab"

- In the "Paragraph ribbon or group", choose Paragraph Settings.

- Click the Tabs button.

- Set the Tab stop position, choose the Alignment and Leader options. By default, your tab stop is always on "0.5", you can also modify that and the positioning alignment with other aspects too, once done, click the "Ok" option and use your "Tab" key to test your text movement spacing.

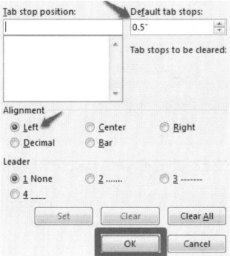

Hyphenating Text

Hyphenation is used when a text runs out of space on a line. With hyphenation, text will automatically move down to the next line. When you turn on hyphenation, the text will hyphenate itself by default when running out of space.

- Go to "Layout tab"

- Under the "Layout tab", below locate "Hyphenation"

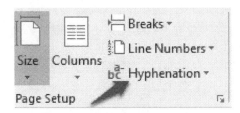

- Once you select "Hyphenation", dropdown options will pop up such as "None", "Automatic", "Manual" and "Hyphenation options"

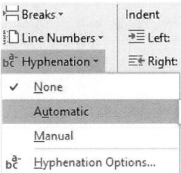

- Once you select "Automatic", it will take effect on your document

Excel allows you to perform complex calculations where changing one number causes many other calculated numbers to change as well. Excel includes an extensive library of built-in formulas to help you perform those calculations.

Automatically and manually hyphenating

Automatic hyphenating keeps all texts hyphenated, while manual hyphenating gives its user access to edit how text should be hyphenated.

CHAPTER SIX

WORD STYLES

All About Styles

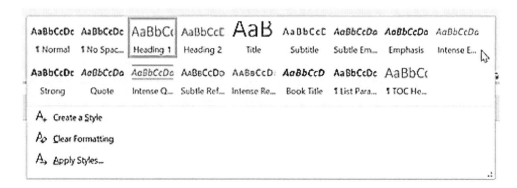

Style is a predefined template used to differentiate between texts such as heading text from body text. Style comes with other options for creating a new style, clearing an existing format, applying styles, and modifying styles.

Style and Templates

Style as said earlier is a predefined template that comes with auto-installed font style, size, and color which makes it a template to be used when the need arises. Note that style, as the name implies is not only for designing text, it can also be used for creating tables of content, headings, and lots more.

Types of Styles

It is important to note that one style is different totally from another with its unique name.

Paragraph styles

Paragraph

These styles control the appearance of a text in paragraph sections and allow you to edit large sections of text. A paragraph style may contain format settings for character style, it's also the overall design of a paragraph. The paragraph style Standard is usually preset for the entire text. Paragraph styles format Indents, and spacings, Line and page breaks, borders and shading, lists, tabs, all character attributes.

Character styles

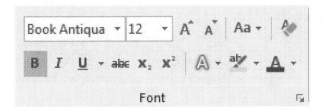

Font

Character style is the appearance of text based on individual choice and is mostly used to format text sections such as highlighting words. Character styles do not format the entire paragraph, but rather, format font, font size, font color, bold, italic, or underlined markings, and so on.

Table styles

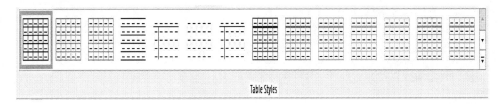

Table Styles

Table styles determine the formatting outlook of your table in terms of individual choice and the purpose of usage can be for creating a calendar, scoring list, items, and lots more.

List styles

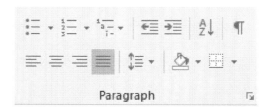

List styles in Word format give the appearance that best suits the user, such as importing an image as 'list style', formatting of bulleted lists, formatting of numbered lists, indents, and lots more.

What are the advantages of Word styles when formatting a text?

Preset as well as custom styles make it easier to work on a text document with simplicity and flexibility. This is mostly visible while editing complex documents. Primarily, manual formatting seems easier and quicker, but for longer texts, it's more effective to use Word styles instead of frequently formatting text sections separately. The advantages of using styles in Word are:

- **Adaptability**
- **Simplicity**
- **Continuity**
- **Efficiency**
- **Navigation**
- **Outlining**

Applying Styles to Text and Paragraphs

- Highlight the text to be altered

Word's for Printing

A Word document is formatted to fit on a specific size page with the text automatically flowing from one page to the next. Excel supports printing, but its page breaks are not obvious, and because it's printing area can extend multiple pages horizontally as well as vertically the page breaks can be difficult to manage.

- Go to the "Home tab" which is your default displayed Word 2019 interface

Home

- At your right-hand side, second to the last, you will see the "Styles" ribbon

- Select one of the styles above, you can also click on the dropdown arrow to view other styles, let's assume we choose "Heading 1"

- Your highlighted text will be converted to the selected style which is "Heading 1"

Word's for Printing

A Word document is formatted to fit on a specific size page with the text automatically flowing from one page to the next. Excel supports printing, but its page breaks are not obvious, and because it's printing area can extend multiple pages horizontally as well as vertically the page breaks can be difficult to manage.

- You can also do something similar to your paragraph by also highlighting it

Word's for Printing

A Word document is formatted to fit on a specific size page with the text automatically flowing from one page to the next. Excel supports printing, but its page breaks are not obvious, and because it's printing area can extend multiple pages horizontally as well as vertically the page breaks can be difficult to manage.

- Go to the "Home tab" which is your default displayed Word 2019 screen

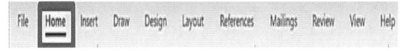

- At your right-hand side, locate the "Style" ribbon

- Now, let select the second heading which is "Heading 2"

- Your paragraph text will change to "Heading 2" styling

Word's for Printing

A Word document is formatted to fit on a specific size page with the text automatically flowing from one page to the next. Excel supports printing, but its page breaks are not obvious, and because it's printing area can extend multiple pages horizontally as well as vertically the page breaks can be difficult to manage.

Experimenting with style sets

- Go to the "Home tab" which is your default displayed Word 2019 screen

- At your right-hand side, locate the "Style" ribbon, click the dropdown arrow as illustrated below to see other options

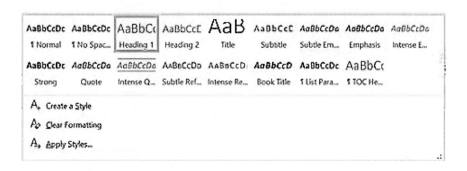

- Below is what you will be shown, you can select your preferred choice, or create your preferred choice; that is how style is applied to text.

Creating a New Style

- Go to the "Home tab"

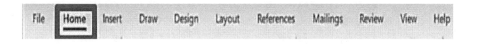

- At your right-hand side, second to the last ribbon, you will see "Styles", select the dropdown arrow as illustrated below

- Different options will be shown to you, among the options choose "Create a Style"

- Another dialog box will pop-up titled "Name", name it according to your choice

- Then, select "Modify" for more modification on your newly created style

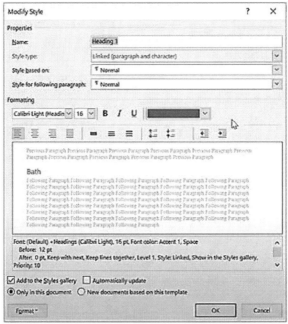

- Once done, click "Ok", your newly created style will be added to the styles list

Modifying styles

Modification is majorly in two ways, you either modify your existing style or your just created style, I just explained **"Creating a New Style"** and I illustrated how to modify it. Here, I will be demonstrating how to modify existing styles

- Go to the "Home tab"

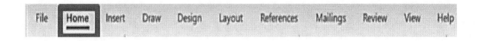

- On your right-hand side, you will see the "Styles" ribbon. Assuming we want to modify "Heading 1", right-click on it, a dialog box will appear with many options, select "Modify"

- Here is where your "Heading 1" modification which is one of the existing styles on your list is. You can modify the font style, font size, boldness, color, and many more. For simplicity and illustration purpose, click on "color" and choose "red" color, then click "Ok".

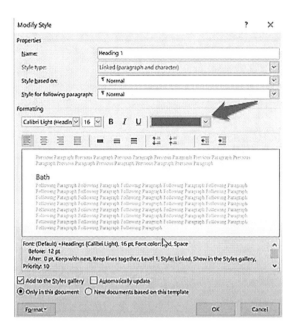

- Note the changes, "Heading 1" which is one of the existing styles will have the effect of color red which we modified it to

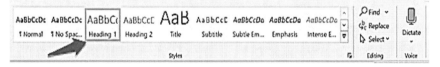

Renaming Styles

- Make sure your text that carries a style format is highlighted to recognize the specific style to be renamed

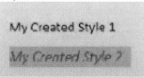

- Go to the "Home tab"

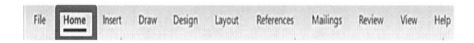

- At your right-hand side, you will see the "styles" ribbon

- Below the "styles" ribbon, click on the little arrow

- A dialog box will appear, indicating your selected or created style

- Below the "Styles displayed box", select the last option titled "Manage Styles". Double-click on "Manage Styles"

- Another dialog box will appear, make sure your style is highlighted as indicated in the illustration below, then click on "Modify"

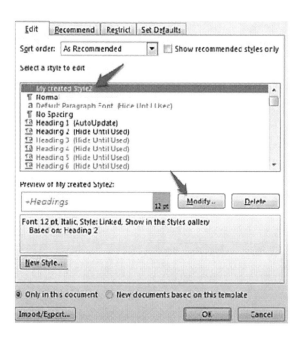

- You will be brought to the modification box named "Properties". This is where your selected style can be edited, renamed, and your font size, style, color, alignment, and the rest can be worked upon. Once done hit "ok"

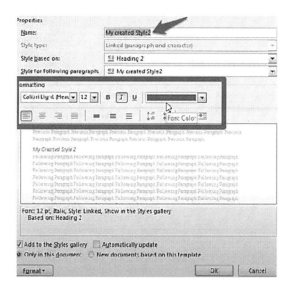

- Let's assume I only renamed my style from "My created Style 2" to "My 2"

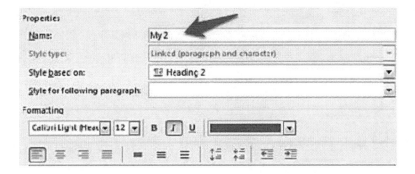

- Once done, click "ok"

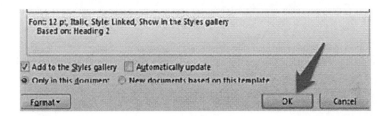

- Your previous displayed box titled "Manage styles" will also affect the new changes, also click "ok" to see your styles ribbon having the same effect

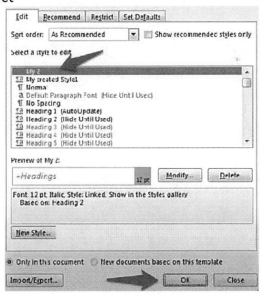

- Now, you will see the changes we made on renaming our style from "My created Style 2" to "My 2"

Applying Themes in Word 2019

Themes is a multiple template design to suit individual preferred choice, its major purpose is to make Word interface stylish in a unique way. Themes, once selected, automatically changes the whole outlook of your content.

How to Apply Themes

- Go to the "Design" tab

- At your left-hand side, select "Themes"

- Drop-down options of themes will be shown to you immediately

- Select your preferred choice. Each theme has its template style

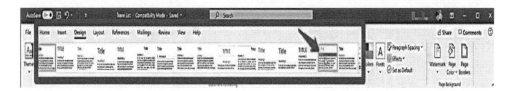

- Assuming we select the above theme where the arrow is pointed, all your headings will also be painted blue color, and any style that was there before will be changed.

CHAPTER SEVEN
CONSTRUCTING A PERFECT TABLE

Table Jargon

A table is a grid of cells arranged in vertical and horizontal order. It is also a great way to organize information within your document. Tables are useful for different activities such as the arrangement of description items, presenting text information and numerical data, text and image illustration, and lots more. In Word, you can create a blank table, convert text to a table, and apply a variety of styles and formats to existing tables.

Creating a Table

Creating a table has been for different purposes such as for grading, calculating, listing of names, items, and so on. To create a table, simply follow this procedure

- Go to the "Insert" tab

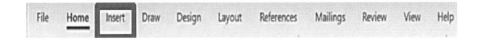

- Below the "Insert tab", you will see "Table", click the little arrow under to get the dropdown table options

- Once you click on the arrow, you get the dropdown rows and columns which is known as "Table Grid". Select the numbers of rows and columns you want, then, click on the last selection of row and column to display it on your Word document

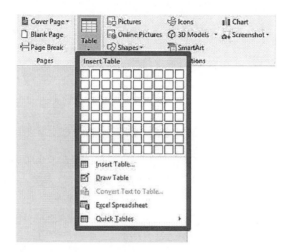

- Assuming we pick five rows and two columns, at the last selection, right-click on your mouse to effect it on your Word document

- Here is the result that you will have on your Word document

Styling your table

- Go to "Insert"

- Below the "Insert tab" you will see "Table", click the little arrow to get the dropdown table options

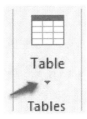

Table

Tables

- Once you click on the arrow, you get the dropdown rows and columns which is known as "Table Grid". Select the numbers of rows and columns, then click on the last selection of row and column to display it on your Word document

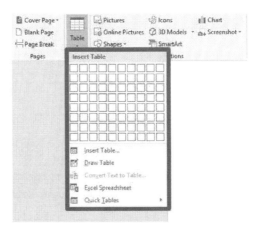

- Once you have selected the number of rows (horizontal) and columns (vertical), then your table will be displayed in your Word document, let's assume it is four rows and three columns

- Click inside one of the columns, once you do this, it becomes active to receive text

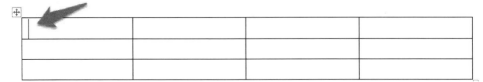

- Immediately, the menu bar will show "Table Tools" which are the "Design" table tab and "Layout" table tab, click on "Design table tab"

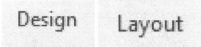

- Under "Design", you will see "table" styles which consist of predefined table styles to use, click on any colorful style to see its effect on your table

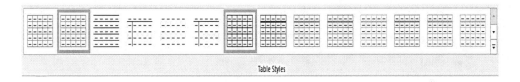

- You can also click on the dropdown arrow on your right-hand side to view other table options

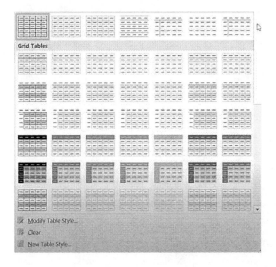

- Once selected, your created table will be transformed into the predefined template

Note: "Table Tools" only show up whenever the table cell is active.

Entering Text and Numbers in your Table

- Go to the "Insert" tab

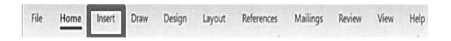

- Below the "Insert tab", you will see "Table", click the little arrow to get the dropdown table options

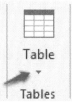

- Once you click on it, you get the "Table Grid", select the numbers of rows and columns you want, then click on the last selection of row and column to display it on your Word document

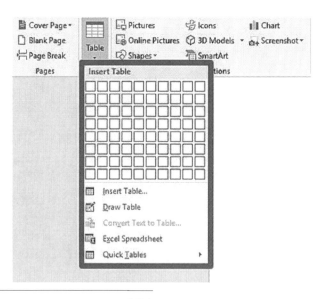

- Once you have selected the number of rows (horizontal) and columns (vertical), then your table will be displayed in your Word document. Assuming it is three rows and five columns, place your mouse cursor on the table to type your text and number

- Then, start typing your words inside

Number	Text	
1	One	
2	Two	
3	Three	
4	Four	

Adding additional rows and columns

- Go to "Insert tab"

File   Home   Insert   Draw   Design   Layout   References   Mailings   Review   View   Help

- There, you will see "Table", click the little arrow to get the dropdown options

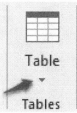

Table

Tables

- Once you click on "Table", you get the "Table Grid", select the numbers of rows and columns you want, then click on the last selection of row and column to display it on your Word document

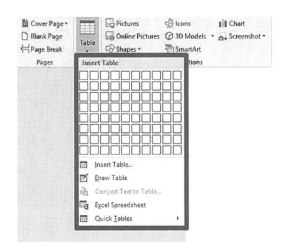

- Once you select the number of rows and columns and you have inputted your texts, there is a possibility of needing an additional table to continue your content, simply place your cursor at the edge of your table as illustrated below.

Position	Type	Location
Computer Engineer	Full-time, two months	Clearwater
Software Developer	Full-time, open-ended	Tampa
UI Designer	Part-time, two months	St. Petersburg

- Once you see the plus sign (+), click on it, another empty single row and column will be created

Position	Type	Location
Computer Engineer	Full-time, two months	Clearwater
Software Developer	Full-time, open-ended	Tampa
UI Designer	Part-time, two months	St. Petersburg

- You can then fill up the empty rows and columns with your desired text

Position	Type	Location
Computer Engineer	Full-time, two months	Clearwater
Project Assistant	Full-time, three months	Coral Springs
Software Developer	Full-time, open-ended	Tampa
UI Designer	Part-time, two months	St. Petersburg

How to use Autofit on Table

Before we go into how to use autofit, what is autofit all about? Autofit is a predefined feature that gives your table the privilege to fit automatically to the text length. How do we use autofit?

- Simply go to "Insert"

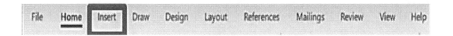

- Below "Insert", you will see "Table", click the little arrow to get the dropdown table options

- Once you click on "Table", you get the "Table Grid

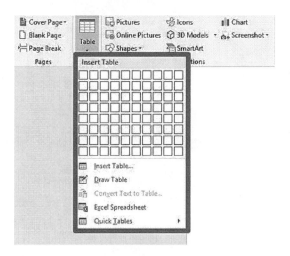

- Create the number of rows and columns for your table, then select it, once it appears on your Word document, you can type your text into it. For us to see how "Autofit" works, I will use my previous table to illustrate "Autofit"

Position	Type	Location
Computer Engineer	Full-time, two months	Clearwater
Project Assistant	Full-time, three months	Coral Springs
Software Developer	Full-time, open-ended	Tampa
UI Designer	Part-time, two months	St. Petersburg

- Once you click any part of your table, a little plus (+) sign will appear on your left-hand side, click on it

Position	Type	Location
Computer Engineer	Full-time, two months	Clearwater
Project Assistant	Full-time, three months	Coral Springs
Software Developer	Full-time, open-ended	Tampa
UI Designer	Part-time, two months	St. Petersburg

- Your table will be automatically highlighted

Position	Type	Location
Computer Engineer	Full-time, two months	Clearwater
Project Assistant	Full-time, three months	Coral Springs
Software Developer	Full-time, open-ended	Tampa
UI Designer	Part-time, two months	St. Petersburg

- Then, look above, you will see "Table Tools" appearing since your table is active. "Table Tools" comes with two options "Design" and "Layout"

- Select "Layout". Under "Layout", look for "Autofit"

AutoFit

- Click on "Autofit" and choose the first option which is "Autofit Contents", once you click on "Autofit Contents"

- Your table will automatically resize to your text contents size, you can compare the previous table and the recent "Autofit" to see the changes in size

Position	Type	Location
Computer Engineer	Full-time, two months	Clearwater
Project Assistant	Full-time, three months	Coral Springs
Software Developer	Full-time, open-ended	Tampa
UI Designer	Part-time, two months	St. Petersburg

Aligning your table positioning

- Simply go to "Insert tab"

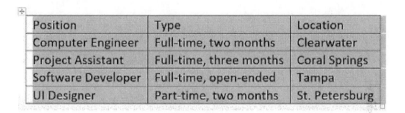

- Below "Insert", you will see "Table", click the little arrow to get the dropdown options

- Once you click on "Table", you get the "Table Grid", select the numbers of rows and columns you want to work with, then click on the last selection of rows and column to display it on your Word document

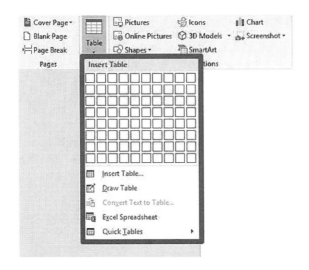

- Once it appears on your Word document, you can type your text into it. For us to see how to align a table, I will use my previous table to illustrate how to align your table

Position	Type	Location
Computer Engineer	Full-time, two months	Clearwater
Project Assistant	Full-time, three months	Coral Springs
Software Developer	Full-time, open-ended	Tampa
UI Designer	Part-time, two months	St. Petersburg

- Once you click any part of your table a little plus (+) sign will appear on your left-hand side, click on it

Position	Type	Location
Computer Engineer	Full-time, two months	Clearwater
Project Assistant	Full-time, three months	Coral Springs
Software Developer	Full-time, open-ended	Tampa
UI Designer	Part-time, two months	St. Petersburg

- All your table will be automatically highlighted

Position	Type	Location
Computer Engineer	Full-time, two months	Clearwater
Project Assistant	Full-time, three months	Coral Springs
Software Developer	Full-time, open-ended	Tampa
UI Designer	Part-time, two months	St. Petersburg

- Then, go to your "home" tab

File   Home   Insert   Draw   Design   Layout   References   Mailings   Review   View   Help

- By your right-hand side under the "Paragraph" ribbon, there are four types of alignment; left alignment, center alignment, right alignment, and justify alignment. For understanding, we will be using center alignment to see the effect, because by default your table is on left alignment; simply click the "**center alignment**" which is the second alignment icon from your left

- You can press the shortcut, "Ctrl + E" on your keyboard, your table will be moved to the center point. Once you select center alignment as illustrated, here's what it will look like

For further information about any of these new jobs, or a complete listing of jobs that are available through the Career Center, please call Mary Walker-Huelsman at (727) 555-0030 or visit our website at www.fpcc.pro/careers.

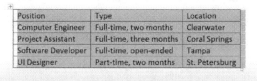

Position	Type	Location
Computer Engineer	Full-time, two months	Clearwater
Project Assistant	Full-time, three months	Coral Springs
Software Developer	Full-time, open-ended	Tampa
UI Designer	Part-time, two months	St. Petersburg

To help prepare yourself before applying for these jobs, we recommend that you review the following articles on our website at www.fpcc.pro/careers.

Manual Way of Inserting a Table

- Simply go to your "Insert tab"

- Under "Insert", locate "Table" and click on it

- A dropdown option will be displayed choose "Insert Table"

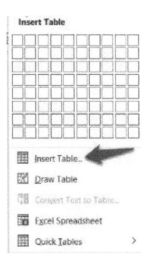

- Another dialog box will appear where you can insert the number of rows and columns to be displayed in your document. By default, manual insert for columns is five, while for rows is two, these can be adjusted at wish. You can also decide to choose "Autofit to contents", "Autofit to window" or "Fixed column width", then, hit "Ok" to effect your changes

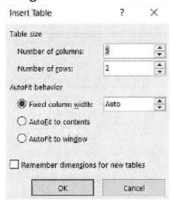

- If you did not edit the manual insert table, below is the result you will get

How to delete columns and rows

- Since I have shown you how to insert tables, now let us look at how to delete or remove that which was inserted. Assuming we have five (5) rows and seven (7) columns, and all we need is only four (4) rows and six (6) columns, simply click on row 7 on the table as an indication of where we want to delete

1.				
2.				
3.				
4.				
5.				
6.				
7.				

- Look above, you will see "Table Design" and "Layout", choose "Layout"

- Under "Layout" on your left-hand side, you will see multiple options on the "Rows & Columns" ribbon such as "Delete", "Insert above", "Insert below", and other options. Click on "Delete"

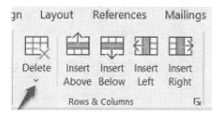

- A dropdown menu will be displayed, select "Delete Rows" from the options, your rows that was seven (7) in number will become six (6)

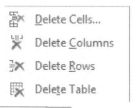

- This should be your result. Note, anywhere your cursor is within your table is where the delete will take effect from

1.				
2.				
3.				
4.				
5.				
6.				

How to Merge Cells in a table & Designing a table style

Beyond explanation, it is also important to understand the little element that the big element is made up of. "Cell" is the inputted part where your text and number are inserted into. So, why merge cells? Merging of cells is mostly needed for various reasons such as naming your table, constructing a calendar.

The month and year (for example, January 2022) need to occupy the first rows in a bold and large format to give a clear update on what the table is all about as seen in the image below

January 2022						
Sunday	Monday	Tuesday	Wednesday	Thursday	Friday	Saturday
						1
2	3	4	5	6	7	8
9	10	11	12	13	14	15
16	17	18	19	20	21	22
23	24	25	26	27	28	29
30	31					

Then, how do we merge cells?

- Since I have shown you how to insert tables, Let's assume we want to create something similar to the calendar format above. For us to merge our table, if you count the rows, you will notice it is seven (7) in number, while the columns are eight (8) in number including the heading (January 2022). This is also an opportunity to create a calendar with Office Word document. After creating your table, input the text and number in its various location

January 2022						
Sunday	Monday	Tuesday	Wednesday	Thursday	Friday	Saturday
						1
2	3	4	5	6	7	8
9	10	11	12	13	14	15
16	17	18	19	20	21	22
23	24	25	26	27	28	29
30	31					

- Then, place your cursor at the beginning of "January 2022"

January 2022						
Sunday	Monday	Tuesday	Wednesday	Thursday	Friday	Saturday
						1
2	3	4	5	6	7	8
9	10	11	12	13	14	15
16	17	18	19	20	21	22
23	24	25	26	27	28	29
30	31					

- Once your cursor is blinking at the beginning of January 2022, simply hold down "Shift key" on your keyboard with the "forward Arrow" at the right-hand side of your keyboard. It will be highlighting your first row, once your highlighting gets to the last row, release your hand from the "Shift & "Arrow keys" on your keyboard, below is where the highlighting of your rows should stop

January 2022						
Sunday	Monday	Tuesday	Wednesday	Thursday	Friday	Saturday
						1
2	3	4	5	6	7	8
9	10	11	12	13	14	15
16	17	18	19	20	21	22
23	24	25	26	27	28	29
30	31					

- After highlighting it, go to the "menu bar", click on "Layout"

File   Home   Insert   Draw   Design   Layout   References   Mailings   Review   View   Help

- Under "Layout" look at your left-hand side, you will see the "Merge" ribbon, click on "Merge cells"

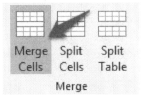

- By default, your highlighted row will be merged as one, you will also notice the column lines that separate the entire table is no longer applicable to the "January 2022" row

January 2022						
Sunday	Monday	Tuesday	Wednesday	Thursday	Friday	Saturday
						1
2	3	4	5	6	7	8
9	10	11	12	13	14	15
16	17	18	19	20	21	22
23	24	25	26	27	28	29
30	31					

Designing a table style

- Now, to make it look fashionable, simply click on "Design"

- Then select your built-in table template, you can click the little dropdown arrow for other options of your choice; remember we want it to look like the blue template shown earlier

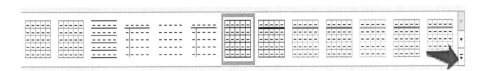

- You will be shown other table design options, the arrangement might be different but the table design remain the same, once you select it, your table will possess the template

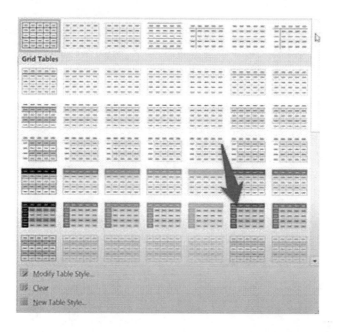

- Now, you see we are closer to what you saw earlier, don't forget to apply "Autofit Content" under "Layout" to make it look professional and similar to what I did, which I also applied into what you are seeing. You can revisit chapter seven to see how to apply "Autofit Content" to your created table

January 2022						
Sunday	Monday	Tuesday	Wednesday	Thursday	Friday	Saturday
						1
2	3	4	5	6	7	8
9	10	11	12	13	14	15
16	17	18	19	20	21	22
23	24	25	26	27	28	29
30	31					

- Now, let us do the final part, make sure your "January 2022" is highlighted. Simply to go your "Home tab" and under the "font" ribbon, select "**Bold**" if yours is not bolded. It is recognized with a **B** icon. Also, increase the "font-size" to "20" to get the same result

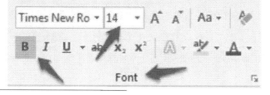

- Then, go to the next ribbon which is the "Paragraph" ribbon, select "center alignment" as illustrated below or you press the shortcut keys "Ctrl + E" from your keyboard to also get the same result

- Your highlighted text which is "January 2022" will move to the center, aligned to the middle, and also increase in size only if it is still highlighted

January 2022						
Sunday	Monday	Tuesday	Wednesday	Thursday	Friday	Saturday
						1
2	3	4	5	6	7	8
9	10	11	12	13	14	15
16	17	18	19	20	21	22
23	24	25	26	27	28	29
30	31					

How to Split Cells in a Table

Splitting of cells means dividing a Cell into multiple cells. Splitting cells is the opposite of merging cells. We will be using our calendar table to illustrate how to split a cell in a table by following these procedures:

- Assuming we are splitting back "January 2022" that was merged, simply highlight "January 2022", and click on "Design" in the menu bar to change its blue displayed design to black & white which is the default table color (black & white has nothing to do with splitting) just for us to be able to see the changes on the splitting of cells

January 2022						
Sunday	Monday	Tuesday	Wednesday	Thursday	Friday	Saturday
						1
2	3	4	5	6	7	8
9	10	11	12	13	14	15
16	17	18	19	20	21	22
23	24	25	26	27	28	29
30	31					

- Once you change your table template back to black & white, as long as you followed the illustration that led to me adding a table template, you get this as your result

January 2022						
Sunday	Monday	Tuesday	Wednesday	Thursday	Friday	Saturday
						1
2	3	4	5	6	7	8
9	10	11	12	13	14	15
16	17	18	19	20	21	22
23	24	25	26	27	28	29
30	31					

- Note that I still highlighted "January 2022" since it's what we merged before. Also, note that you can also split other areas of your table rows and columns which I will be illustrating soon. To proceed with the splitting, simply go to "Layout" on your menu bar

- Then, select "Split Cells"

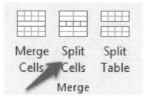

- A dialog box will appear, asking for how many rows and columns you want the highlighted area to multiply into. Note, your button might not be like the illustration below, depending on your operating system, therefore, don't be surprised by any changes you observe

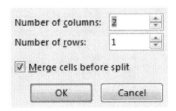

Number of columns: 2

Number of rows: 1

☑ Merge cells before split

OK   Cancel

- Choose your preferred number, assuming we want to use the default numbering which is 2 columns and 1 row, your selection will reflect on your result and the highlighted "January 2022" will be moved to one cell since another cell has been created, but it will still maintain its alignment and other features format applied to it

January 2022						
Sunday	Monday	Tuesday	Wednesday	Thursday	Friday	Saturday
						1
2	3	4	5	6	7	8
9	10	11	12	13	14	15
16	17	18	19	20	21	22
23	24	25	26	27	28	29
30	31					

Moving columns and rows

It is possible to move your table around to any location on your document by simply following this simple step:

- For comprehensive understanding, let us use our created calendar table. As explained earlier, point your mouse cursor into your table in the next cell after number "31" as illustrated below, then, a plus (+) sign will appear at the top left corner, use your mouse cursor to hold it down and drag it to anywhere you want to place it within your document.

January 2022						
Sunday	Monday	Tuesday	Wednesday	Thursday	Friday	Saturday
						1
2	3	4	5	6	7	8
9	10	11	12	13	14	15
16	17	18	19	20	21	22
23	24	25	26	27	28	29
30	31					

Decorating your table with borders and colors

Borders are the lines that form table edges. With borders, you can decorate your table and design it to your preferred choice. How to decorate your table with borders and colors will be explained step by step below

- To save time because of the process of creating another table, we will be using our calendar table. Highlight your heading cell which is "January 2022" or you point your cursor into the "January 2022" row. Note you can use any cell, just for a well-ordered work, we will use the heading cell (January 2022)

Sunday	Monday	Tuesday	Wednesday	Thursday	Friday	Saturday
						1
2	3	4	5	6	7	8
9	10	11	12	13	14	15
16	17	18	19	20	21	22
23	24	25	26	27	28	29
30	31					

January 2022

- Then, the table options will appear named "Table tools", under it is "Design" and "Layout", click on "Layout"

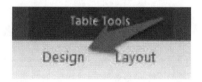

- At your right-hand side, locate "Borders"

- Click on "Borders" to select a different line style format to replace the default borders. For example, we could choose a triple line border

- We can also change the line weight to one and a half point ($1\frac{1}{2}$ pt)

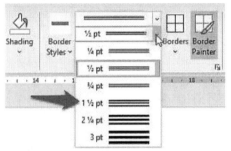

- We can also change the border color by picking the orange color

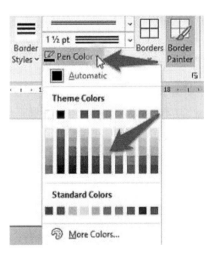

- Once your color has been selected, the "Border Styles", "Line Weight", "Line Styles" and "Pen Color" will have the effect of your chosen color. Note that your "Border Painter" is selected automatically

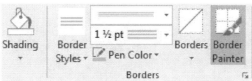

- Once your "Border Painter" is selected, your mouse cursor will change to pen cursor, simply place it on the line edge you want your triple line and color to affect. Note, if you place it wrongly, you will need to select "Border Painter" again

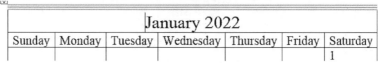

January 2022						
Sunday	Monday	Tuesday	Wednesday	Thursday	Friday	Saturday
						1

- But there is also another way out without having to click and wrongly place line edges; simply click on "Borders"

- Then, select what area you want your border to cover such as "Bottom Border", "Top Border", "Left Border", "Right Border" and so on. We will be clicking on "All Borders"

- Once "All Borders" has been selected, your created calendar table will be formatted on your active cell which is "January 2022" where your mouse cursor is pointing.

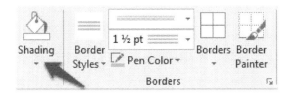

NOTE: If you want the remaining rows and columns to also be formatted, then, you need to highlight the entire table to perform such an operation.

- You can also add shade color on the background of "January 2022" by changing the white background. To do this, click on "Shading"

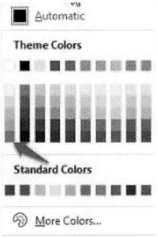

- Select your preferred color. For illustration, I will pick the gray color to achieve a color blend.

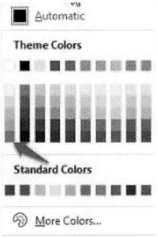

- Your outcome if you choose the same color with me, will be the illustration below

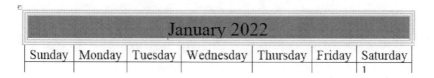

Exploring more on Borders

In continuation of **"Decorating your table with borders and colors"**. It is important to note that there is also more to Border Style

- Still on our created calendar table illustration

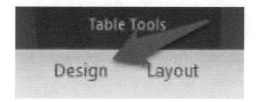

- Click on "Design" table tools

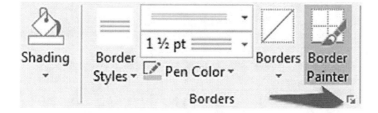

- At your left-hand side, you will see a dropdown arrow, click on it

- You will be brought here, where all our formatted styles are reviewed and edited. It consists of "Borders settings", "Page Border settings" and "Shading settings". If you remember, previously, we choose an orange color, that is why you are seeing orange color and one and half width. Click on the "Shading" option

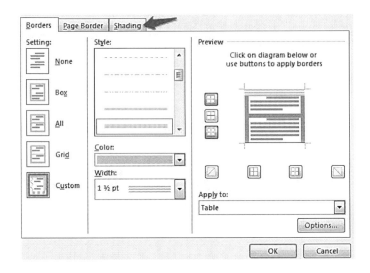

- Once you click on "Shading", you will be brought to this page, where you can set your "Shading Patterns", "Style", "Color" and "Apply to". Under "Apply to", select "Table", then click "Ok" to see the effect

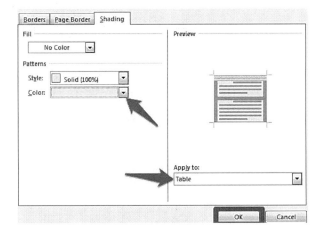

- Here is what your result will be if you do exactly as I did

January 2022						
Sunday	Monday	Tuesday	Wednesday	Thursday	Friday	Saturday
						1
2	3	4	5	6	7	8
9	10	11	12	13	14	15
16	17	18	19	20	21	22
23	24	25	26	27	28	29
30	31					

Using Math Formulas in Tables

This is the unbelievable part of Word; many thinks once you want to do any mathematical calculation you need to use other Microsoft products such as Excel to be able to do your calculation. Every Microsoft App has its uniqueness but can interchange some features within such other since all the applications are all Microsoft packages. Sooner or later, everything will come together uniquely, just as there is now "My Add-ins" that gives other apps the privilege to interact with the Word environment.

So, how do we use mathematical formulas in our table? Below is the step-by-step procedure on how to go about it

- Create a table format as taught earlier, type the below information

Mick Scores	
Math	60
English	80
ICT	55
Physics	75
Total	

- Once done, click your mouse cursor directly to your empty cell which is where your total summation will be, make sure your mouse cursor is blinking on the empty cell for your summation

Mick Scores	
Math	60
English	80
ICT	55
Physics	75
Total	

- Now, go to "Layout" in your menu bar, click on it

File   Home   Insert   Draw   Design   Layout   References   Mailings   Review   View   Help

- Look at the last tool on your right-hand side you will see "Formula" with an "fx" icon, click on it

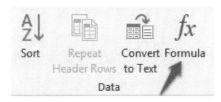

- A dialog box will appear, with a default formula "=SUM(ABOVE)" *=SUM, represent add up (+) your figures together. (ABOVE) represent add the numbers in the column above the cell you are in. (LEFT) represent add the numbers in the row to the left side of the cell you're in. (BELOW) represent add the numbers in the column below the cell you're in. (RIGHT) represent adds the numbers in the row to the right side of the cell you are in.*
  Your "Number format" represents your figure settings. For example, $100 can be $100.00 depending on how you want your number format to look.

Your "Paste function" is an added formula feature by Microsoft to perform more complex calculations by default. You can just click the "Ok" option to just perform your normal summing calculation.

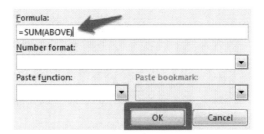

- Your "Mick Scores" will be summed up automatically

Mick Scores	
Math	60
English	80
ICT	55
Physics	75
Total	270

How to move or drag a table

- Assuming we are using the "Mick Scores" table,

Mick Scores	
Math	60
English	80
ICT	55
Physics	75
Total	270

- Place your mouse cursor on any cell, mine was placed on the "total score 270", a little plus (+) sign will appear at the left side, use your mouse cursor to pin it down then drag it to any position on your document

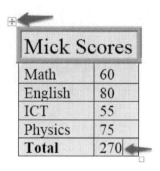

Mick Scores	
Math	60
English	80
ICT	55
Physics	75
Total	270

How to enlarge or reduce your table

- Assuming we want to enlarge the "Mick Scores" table

Mick Scores	
Math	60
English	80
ICT	55
Physics	75
Total	270

- Click on any cell in your table, for illustration, I will change my mouse cursor from "Total Scores" to "Mick Scores" which is the heading. Once your mouse cursor is blinking in any cell you choose, you will notice additional features joint together with your table, one is your top left cross arrow which has been discussed, while the other is a "little white box" below your table on the right-hand side as indicated with a pink arrow.

Mick Scores	
Math	60
English	80
ICT	55
Physics	75
Total	270

- Once you hold down the "little white box" with your mouse cursor, drag it down to enlarge it or upward to reduce it.

Enlarged

Mick Scores	
Math	60
English	80
ICT	55
Physics	75
Total	270

Reduced

Mick Scores	
Math	60
English	80
ICT	55
Physics	75
Total	270

Using a picture as the table background

- Let's create an empty table as you were taught earlier by checking on the "Insert" tab to locate your "Table" and create columns and rows

- Next, insert text inside your cells, type "Island", "Animal" and "Nature" on each cell by your left-hand side

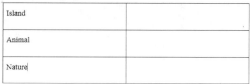

- Now, place your mouse cursor in the first empty cell on the right side

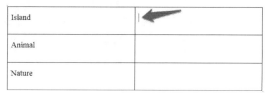

- Make sure your cursor is blinking, then go to your "Insert tab"

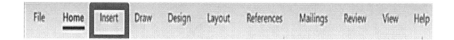

- In the "Insert tab", you will see the "Illustrations" ribbon, select "Pictures" which is the first option

- You will be directed into your PC storage to locate the location of your picture manually, after getting it, then select it and click on the "Insert button" below. Note, you can also get the same image I used as long as you are running Microsoft operating system just go to your "Picture's folder"

- Once your picture has been selected and inserted, the cell where your mouse cursor is blinking will display the picture. Note your picture might increase the table size, simply reduce it by 'reducing the little arrow dot', you can also rotate your picture by moving the curved arrow at the top of the picture

- Let's do the same to the other two empty cells

- Looking at it, you will notice it wasn't properly positioned, this is where additional adjustment is needed; simply click on any cell to make the little plus (+) arrow appear at the top left-hand side

- Once done, click on the plus (+) arrow above, all your table cells will be highlighted

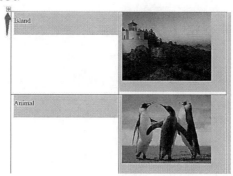

- Then, in your menu bar, and click on "Layout"

- Make sure your table cell is still highlighted, then under "Layout" you will see the "Alignment" ribbon, select "Align Center" which is the middle icon, click on it

- All your entire table cells will automatically be centralized; you can compare the previous table with this adjusted table and see the difference

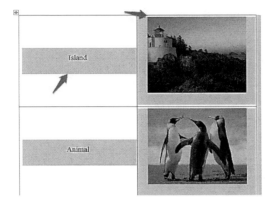

Drawing a table

- Go to "Insert tab"

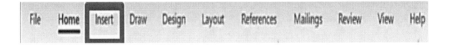

- Under the "Insert tab", select "Table"

- It will display the "Table Grid", under it, select "Draw Table"

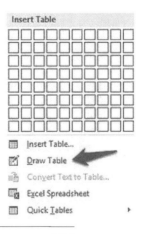

- You can design your table as desired as seen in the illustration below

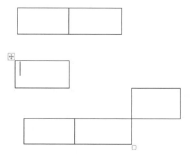

Drawing diagonal lines on tables

- You can draw any table of your choice and also add additional lines into your table as illustrated below. Note that your cursor will always change to a pen icon whenever you are working with the "Draw Table" Tool

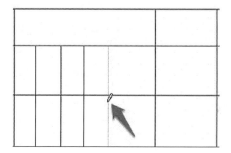

Wrapping text around a table

- Create a table of your choice as you were taught earlier, you can decide to replicate the one I'm using for illustration, two (2) rows, and three (3) columns. Make sure your cursor is blinking inside the one cell

- Next, look above and locate "Table tools". Under "Table Tools", click on "Layout"

- Then, locate "Properties" and click on it

- Once you click on "Properties", a dialog box will be opened titled "Table" properties, under "Table", locate "Text wrapping", by default it is on "None", simply select "Around" and then press "Ok"

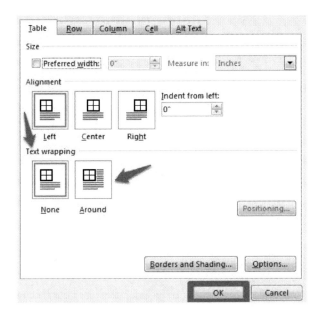

- Then, you can move your table to the center position and start typing or you can drag it into the middle of a text without having any issue with it, just as in the illustration below

A Word document is formatted to fit on a specific size page with the text automatically flowing from one page to the next. Excel supports printing, but its page breaks are not obvious, and because it's printing area can extend multiple pages horizontally as well as vertically the page breaks can be difficult to manage.

Tips

Now you see and understand how flexible and simplified Word 2019 is. Simply do something different from what we have achieved, and let see how comprehensive you get what has been explained to you so far.

CHAPTER EIGHT

TAKING ADVANTAGE OF THE PROOFING TOOLS

Correcting Your Spelling Errors

Computer software such as Word processing has been a wonderful tool for effective means of simplifying human needs. While trying to construct words, typographical errors can occur, this led Microsoft corporation to look for a means to reduce the possibility of typographical errors while typing. Luckily, Word comes with several and different tools that can help you proofread your document and correct any mistake. Many don't know how helpful Word 2019 is when it comes to autocorrect and spelling checking. To know how to autocorrect or scan your document against typographical errors, simply follow this step-by-step procedure below:

- Make sure you are currently on your document to be corrected

- Go to the "Review" tab

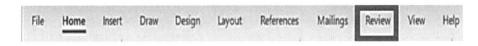

- At your left-hand side, look for "Spelling & Grammar" and click on it

A dialog box will appear on your right-hand side which will start spelling check from the first error to the last, the first typographical error was "Resoucres" instead of "Resources", so if it was intentionally typed, you click on the "Ignore" option. If not, select the corrected word in the suggestion box, then click on the "Change" option to continue to autocorrect other words.

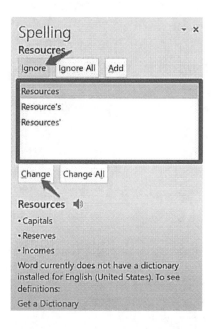

- Once you are done selecting the right suggested words, click on the "Change" option which will take you to the next misspelled text. In this illustration, the next is "Marcom", instead of "Marcum". Note that if the dictionary feature is installed on your Word 2019 and it is a similar word in the dictionary, it will be explained below, if not, click on the "Get a Dictionary" option.

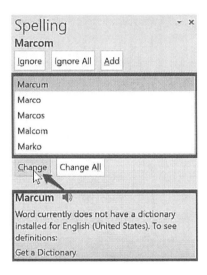

- It is important to note that the spell-checker is not perfect, sometimes it will say a word is spelled wrong when it is not, such as people's names, street names, and other unique proper nouns. If that happens, you have a couple of different options;
  - The **"Ignore"** option will skip the word one time without changing it.
  - The **"Ignore All"** option will skip the word every time it appears in your document.
  - While the **"Add"** option will add the word to your inbuilt dictionary permanently, so it never comes up as an error again. Just make sure the word is spelled correctly before you go with any of these options.

Correcting misspellings one at a time

- By default, Word is designed to mark spelling and grammar errors while you type, that is what the little red and blue wavy lines as seen in the illustration are for, so, you can check your document manually (like I have just shown you), or you can refer to the marks, and make corrections as you go.

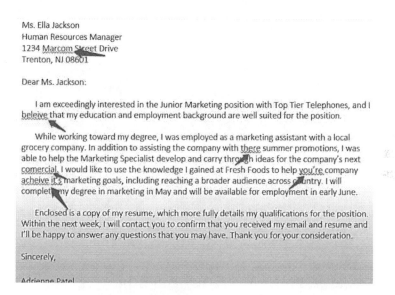

- Red means that there is a spelling error. To correct it, all you have to do is to right-click, then choose the proper spelling from the appeared menu after which the red curly line will be erased.

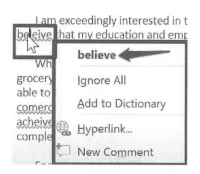

- Here is the corrected text "believe" instead of "beleive"

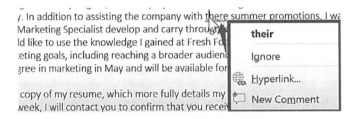

Dear Ms. Jackson:

I am exceedingly
believe that my edu

While working t

- Blue means that there is a kind of grammatical error. In this example, it looks like I used the wrong word in the context of the sentence. I should have used ***"their"*** instead of "there"

y. In addition to assisting the company with there summer promotions, I wa
Marketing Specialist develop and carry throug
ld like to use the knowledge I gained at Fresh Fo
eting goals, including reaching a broader audienc
gree in marketing in May and will be available for

copy of my resume, which more fully details my
week, I will contact you to confirm that you recei

their

Ignore

Hyperlink...

New Comment

Customizing Spelling & Grammar Check

"Word" can be pretty good at picking up on errors like this, but there are certain things that it is set to ignore by default, including sentence fragments, poor sentence structure, and other common grammar mistakes. To include these things in your grammar check, you will need to adjust the default proofing settings. To do this,

- Go to the "Backstage view" which can be accessed through your "File menu"

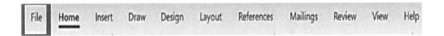

File | Home | Insert | Draw | Design | Layout | References | Mailings | Review | View | Help

- Click on "Options" in the left pane

Account

Feedback

Options

- Then, navigate to "Proofing" in the dialog box

- To customize your grammar settings, look for "Writing Style" near the bottom of the Window. Then click the "settings" option located on the right side

- And another dialog box will appear, here you can choose to set it to check Grammar Only, or Grammar & Style, which will cause Word to be strict about the style of your preferred choice. You can also turn specific items on or off to better suit your needs, for example, if you want Word to check for sentence fragments and run-ons, you can turn them on. Make sure you click the "Ok" button once you are through with the changes.

Preventing text from being spell-checked

- To do this, go to the "Backstage view" which can be accessed through your "File menu"

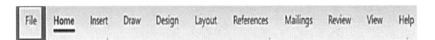

- Click on "Options" in the left pane

- Then, navigate to "Proofing" in the dialog box

- There are still lots of other ways that you can use to customize your settings depending on your preference. For instance, you can stop Word from marking spelling and grammar errors while you type.

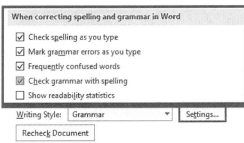

- You can also turn off frequently confused words, like *"**there** vs. **their**".* Keep in mind, your spelling and grammar choices only apply to your copy of Word. So, if you ignore any error, or add a word to your dictionary (for example, your name), those wavy lines will reappear when you send the document to someone else. You can avoid this issue by hiding spelling and grammar errors in this particular document. Just check the two boxes near the bottom of the Window. When you are done, click "Ok" and now, the errors are hidden.

Finding and Replacing Text

Finding and replacing text is one of the Word features that give the privilege to replace text by finding it within a bunch of text without any complication, to know how to find and replace words, follow these simple procedures:

- Go to the *"Home"* tab

- Under the *"Home"* tab, kindly locate *"Replace"* click it or press *"Ctrl + H"*

- A dialog box will appear, enter the word or phrase you want to locate in the *"Find what"* textbox. Also, in the *"Replace with"* textbox, enter the text or phrase you want what you found to be replaced with. For example, I can search for "Thank you" and replace it with "Thanks" on my document.

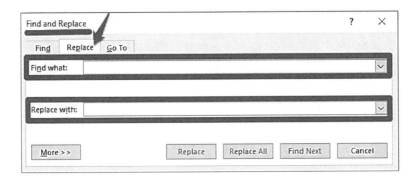

- To update all instances at once, choose "Replace All"

Finding the Right Word with the Thesaurus

Before I explain how to use "Thesaurus", it is important to know what "Thesaurus" is. Thesaurus is a tool that is specially designed into Word by Microsoft for getting the synonyms of whatsoever you are looking for by giving you a bunch of suggestions. For example, you can look for "benefit" and you will be given multiple suggestions of synonyms for "benefit" such as "advantage", "profit", with a classification of which part of speech such words fall under.

Now, how do we make use of Thesaurus? Simply follow these steps:

- Go to your "View" tab"

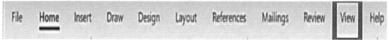

- Under the "View" tab, at your left-hand side, locate "Thesaurus" and double-click on it

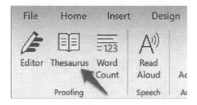

- A dialog box will appear at your right-hand side opposite your Navigation pane dialog box which is located at your left-hand side if activated

- Then, you can type your word or phrase into the "Search" bar. For example, we can look for "Environment" on our "Thesaurus pane" and see what our result will be. You can also type another word of your choice and also see what your result will be

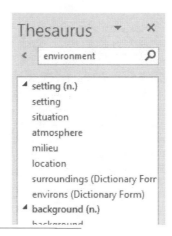

167

Proofing & Converting Text Written in a Foreign Language

- Go to your "Review" tab

- Under the "Review" tab, at your left-hand side, click on "Translate", this will allow you to translate your content into different languages of your choice

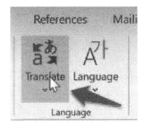

- Now, once you click on "Translate", you will be given two options, one is the "Translate Selection" which enables you to select the specific part of your document to be translated, while the other option is the "Translate Document" which creates a translated copy of your document with Microsoft Translator

- Assuming you select "Translate Selection", a dialog box will appear at the right-hand side where you can select your text or type it inside in the provided textbox

- Let also assume that I select a portion from my text

Hello Anna and Jacob,

Thanks so much for the wonderful book! It was very thoughtful of you two. We have been reading the book to Thomas every single night. He's a very sweet boy and we're very lucky that he's healthy. He'll turn 5 months old on the 14th of June. When we visit Germany, we'll introduce you to Thomas.

Best regards,
Kevin, Kerry, and Thomas

- It will automatically reflect on my translator pane. From English to German based on what I selected. To make use of other languages, click on the present language it will show you other language options

- You can also translate the whole paragraph

Hello Anna and Jacob,

Thanks so much for the wonderful book! It was very thoughtful of you two. We have been reading the book to Thomas every single night. He's a very sweet boy and we're very lucky that he's healthy. He'll turn 5 months old on the 14th of June. When we visit Germany, we'll introduce you to Thomas.

Best regards,
Kevin, Kerry, and Thomas

- Your text will also be interpreted

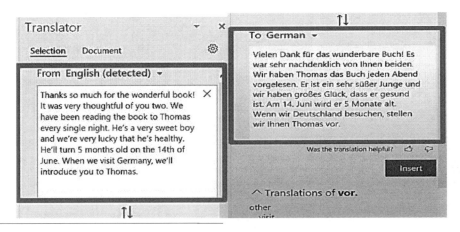

- Then, you can copy the translated copy by highlighting it, right-click, and pick the "copy" option.

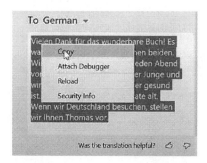

- This can also be pasted into your document.

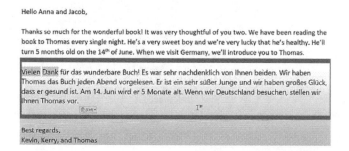

- Let's also see the other option which is "Translate Document". Just click on the other side of your "Translate pane" which is "Document", an instruction of what it is- "Create a translated copy of this document with the Microsoft Translator service" will be written below. Always note that you can change your language anytime you wish by clicking on the current language to select your choice.

- Once you click on "Translate", it will process the translation of your document. Note that you must be connected to the internet via modem, router, Wi-Fi or any means of connection for it to work effectively without bouncing back.

- It will be converted to "German" which is the selected language. Note, the translated document will be opened on a "New document" and your original document will be intact.

- Once completed, check the new document to see the translated document

Hallo Anna und Jakob,

Vielen Dank für das wunderbare Buch! Es war sehr nachdenklich von Ihnen beiden. Wir haben Thomas das Buch jeden Abend vorgelesen. Er ist ein sehr süßer Junge und wir haben großes Glück, dass er gesund ist. Am[14.] Juni wird er 5 Monate alt. Wenn wir Deutschland besuchen, stellen wir Ihnen Thomas vor.

Beste Grüße,
Kevin, Kerry und Thomas

- You can minimize one for the other to preview

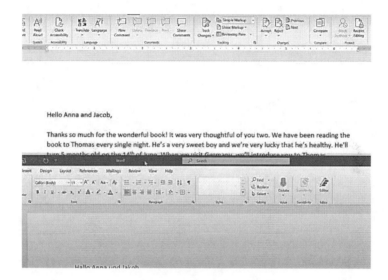

Making use of the Navigation Pane

For simplicity and flexibility, it is important to note that you can have your search bar pane through navigation pane side by side while typing in Word environment, simply follow these step-by-step procedures to achieve that:

- Go to the "View" tab

- Under the "View" tab, at your left-hand side look for "Navigation Pane" make sure it is ticked, if not, do so to see the effect on your document.

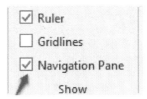

- Here is the result; the below "Navigation" dialog box will automatically appear on the left-hand side of your document permanently except you untick it from the "View" tab. It enables you to see your listed "Headings", slide "Pages", and search "Result" instantly.

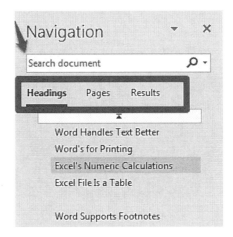

Choosing Language Option

- Go to the "File menu"

- At the displayed interface, click on "Options"

- A dialog box will appear on your left-hand side, select "Language"

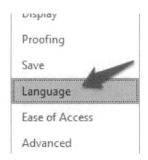

- Then, "Language" features will also appear on your right-hand side, below towards your left-hand side is the "Display Language" option, while at your right-hand side is the "Help Language" option. You can choose from the available languages by scrolling through to see other options.

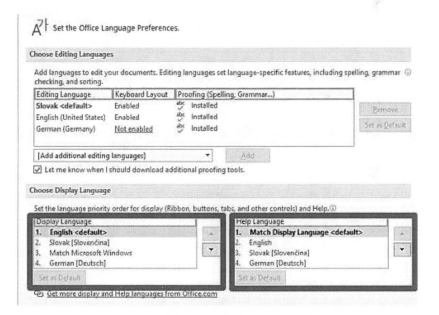

- Once done press, the "Ok" option

- Then, you will be instructed to restart Office so that your language changes can take effect.

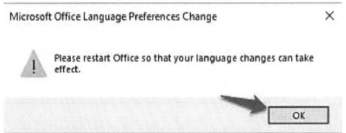

- Take note of your Word 2019 interface before restarting your PC, it's by default in the English language

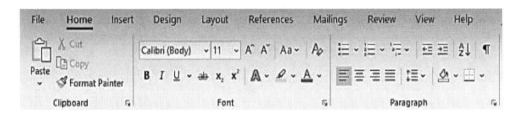

- And here will be the outcome after your PC has been restarted, everything will automatically be in the German language.

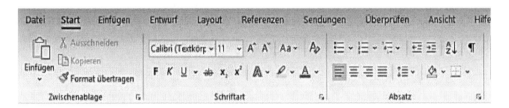

CHAPTER NINE
DESKTOP PUBLISHING WITH WORD

Experimenting with Theme

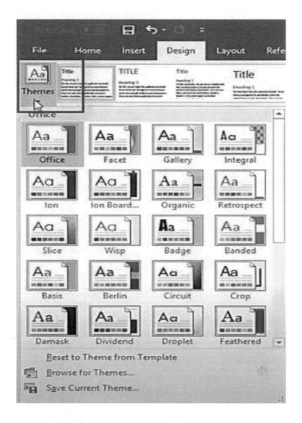

Themes are a predefined style template format that adds to your document content. Each theme uses a unique set of colors, fonts, and effects to create a consistent look. To access your various themes, all you have to do is to go to the "Design" tab, on your right-hand side you will see the word "Themes", click on it and you will be shown different unique themes interface to pick from and each theme as sub-template format.

Decorating a page with a border

• Go to the "Design" tab

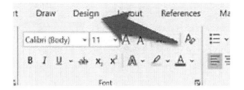

- Under "Design", at your right-hand side, you will see the "Page Background" ribbon, select "Page Borders"

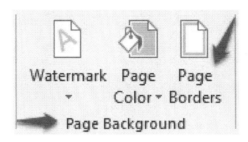

Watermark   Page   Page
   ▼   Color ▼ Borders

Page Background

- Once you click on "Page Borders", a dialog box will pop up which is your "Page Border" configuration. On the left-hand side is the "Setting" option for various page border templates. By the side of the "Setting" option is the "Style" option where you can choose the kind of lines you prefer. Below "Style" is the "Color" option where you can determine which color fits into your page document border.

Below the "Color" option is the "Width" option which is the only component that controls the border thickness. Below the "Width" option is the "Art" option that reflects different kinds of art designs to be used for your framework, while at your right-hand side is the "Preview" option which gives you what your outcome configuration will look like before you click on the "Ok" option.

The "Apply to" option is where you determine where your effect should take place such as "Whole document", "This section", "This section first page only", and "This section all except the first page." Your choice determines your outcome, once done hit the "Ok" button to see your changes.

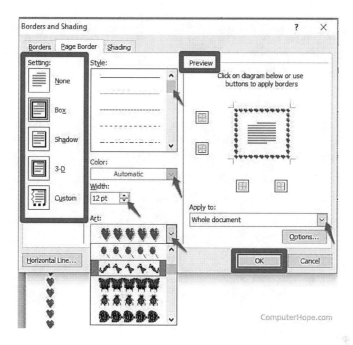

Putting a Background Color on Pages

- In the menu bar, click on "Design"

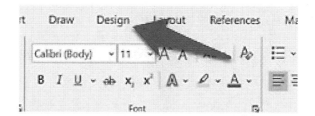

- Under "Design", at your right-hand side, you will see the "Page Background" ribbon, select "Page Color"

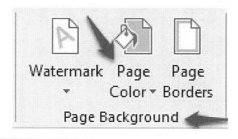

- Under "Page Color", a dropdown box will appear with different kinds of colors. If your preferred color was not found, there's a "More Colors" option below, click on it

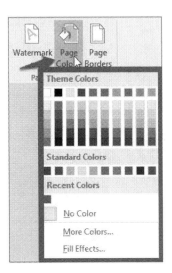

- After clicking the "More Colors" option, you will be brought here under "Standard" where you can randomly select your preferred color which was not found on the page displayed color. On your right-hand side is where your chosen color will be previewed. If you previously choose a color, it will be shown as "Current" with that color, while the newly selected will be shown as "New" with the color you selected as illustrated below.

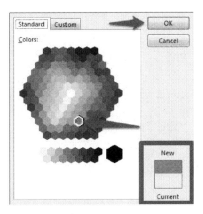

- You can also explore more colors on "Custom" which is an advanced color selection option where you can see the mixture of Colors Red, green, and Blue that was added together to make your preferred color. The illustration below shows that "Yellow color" was picked, and the mixture of it was calculated underneath as "Red: 221", "Green: 221", and "Blue: 35" which resulted in the color yellow.
- **Note** also that beside the color picker, there is a black arrow (◀) which is used for adjustment of any preferred color, once done click the "Ok" button.

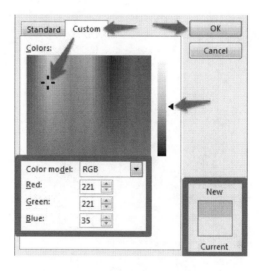

Getting Word 2019 help with Resume Assistant

With Word 2019, there are limitless possibilities to what you can access, that is why I am glad that you made the right choice for purchasing this valuable book which enables you to know some hidden features of Word 2019. It is important to note that Word 2019 has made it possible for third-party software to partner with them for flexibility and simplicity of technology advancement in our day-to-day life. To make Word 2019 assist you with cover letters, simply follow these procedures

- Go to the "Review" tab

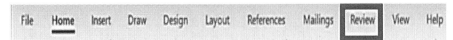

- Under the "Review" tab, look at your right-hand side, you will see "Resume Assistant", click on it

- A dialog box will appear on your right-hand side, click on "Get started" to proceed

- Another way to create a "Resume" is to go to your "file menu", click it

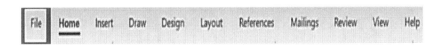

- Click on "New", then, you will be shown multiple template options to pick from, or you can also search online, this will require a data connection

- You can also scroll down to see other "resume" options

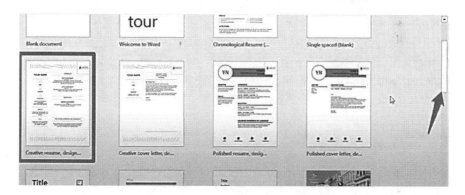

- Once you find your preferred choice, select it and see more information about it, then you can click on "Create"

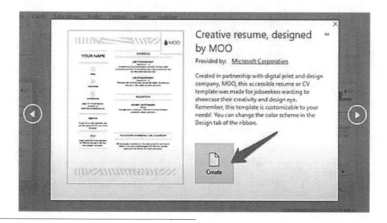

- Once you click on "Create" it will automatically create a template on your Word 2019 for you to work on, and your "Resume Assistant" will also appear on your right-hand side for further assistance

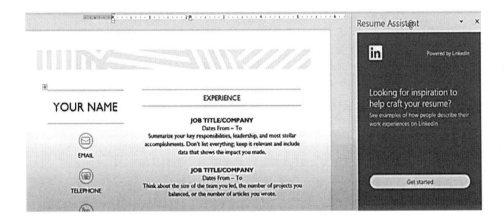

- At your right-hand side on your "Resume Assistant", you can click on "See examples" to see the role and industry format you are looking for

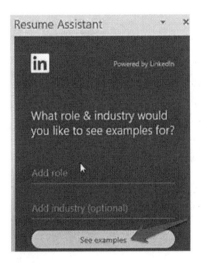

- Or you can go to https://www.linkedin.com/ (this is optional) which is a third-party affiliation to Microsoft. Once you get to the website, you either "Sign in" with your "Linkedin" account or you "Join now" to register afresh. Never enter your Microsoft account details, remember it is a third-party affiliation not owned by Microsoft.

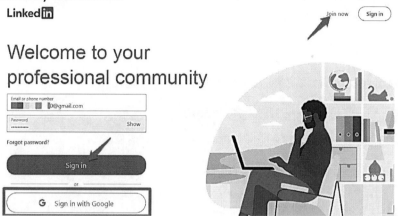

- To join, click on "Join now" at your top right-hand side as illustrated above, then a new page will be brought to you to fill up your registration form

- And if you already have an existing account with "Linkedin", enter it by clicking on the "Sign in" option to explore more on the third-party website, which is specifically designed for professional life where you can showcase what you are up to professionally, and it's also a way of meeting people around the world.

Getting Word 2019 help with cover letters

- Go to your "file menu" click it

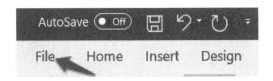

- Click on "New", then, you will be shown multiple template options to pick from or you can also search online, this will require a data connection

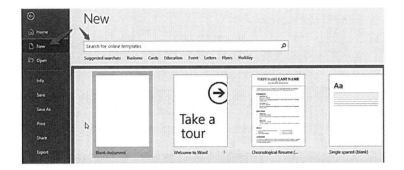

- You can also scroll down to see other "cover letter" options or type "cover letter"

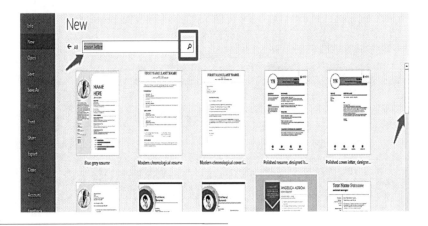

- Once you locate your preferred choice, select it, a pop-up box will appear where you can create it.

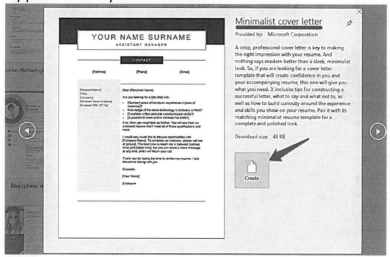

Making Use of Charts, Shapes, and Photos

- Go to your "Insert" tab

- Under the "Insert" tab, locate the "Illustrations" ribbon

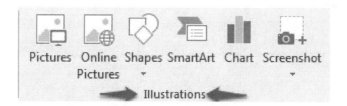

Before we proceed, let's begin by defining "Chart".

What is a Chart?

In a simple word, Chart is a spotted pattern and trend in data used to estimate the graphical scaling by inserting a bar, area, or line chart.

How to Insert "Chart"

- Select "Chart" in the "Illustrations" ribbon

- A dialog box will appear consisting of the "All Charts" features such as "Column", "Line", "Pie", "Bar", "Area", and other charts. It's majorly used to view the estimation of data after it has been concluded.

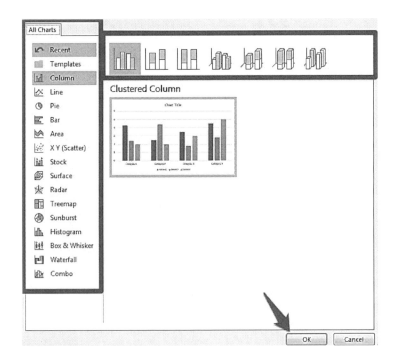

What is a Shape?

Shapes are predefined tools that are used for different purposes such as block arrows shapes, start and banner shapes, equation shapes, and others. To make use of "Shapes", follow these simple procedures below:

- Go to your "Insert tab"

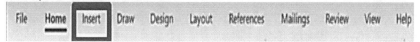

- Under the "Insert" tab, locate "Illustrations", in the "Illustration" ribbon, you will see "Shapes", click on it

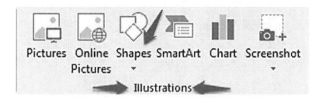

- "Shapes" will show its dropdown features where you can select from. Let's assume we select "love shape" under "Basic Shapes" where my mouse cursor is pointing.

- Once the love shape has been selected, you can now double-click and drag your mouse cursor to make it more visible.

- You can also add more touch to your "love shape" by making sure your mouse cursor is placed on your "love shape", thereby, showing dots around it

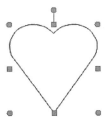

- Then, look above, you will see "Format", click on it

- And you will be shown different colors. You can also click on the dropdown arrow as indicated below to also see other options

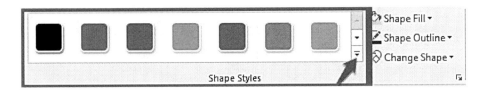

- Select your preferred choice and it will automatically take effect on your selected "love shape".

Now, let talk about Photos which is also known as Pictures

What is a Picture?

A Picture is a static image used for different illustrations and purposes. Now, how do we insert pictures into our Word document?

- Go to "Insert" in your menu bar

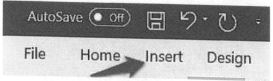

- Under the "Insert" tab, locate the "Illustrations" ribbon. In the "Illustrations" ribbon, select "Pictures"

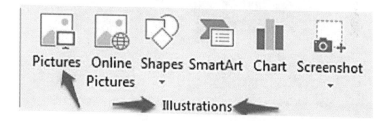

- Once you click on "Pictures", a dialog box will pop up and direct you to your PC storage, locate the folder where your pictures are stored and click on your preferred image, then click "Insert"

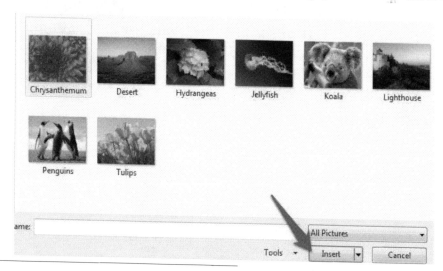

- Then, your image which is also the same as a picture will reflect on your Word document immediately. If you remember earlier when treating how to make use of "Table", I taught you how to resize your image at the dots areas and rotate it if need be, using the curved arrow icon as illustrated below

Positioning and Wrapping Objects Relative to the Page and Text

Positioning and wrapping objects to the page and text can be achieved with the help of "Text Box", which is another hidden feature. Many times, we come across some impossible mathematical images in students' textbooks and keep wondering how did this happen? It is simple, it happens with the help of Word unknown tools. With "Text Box", you can position your words in any area of your document by wrapping your content into it and place it wherever you want your text to be fixed. Then, how do we locate "Text Box"?

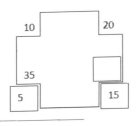

Working with Text Boxes

- Go to the menu bar, select the "Insert" tab

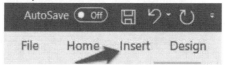

- Under the "Insert" tab, at your right-hand side, look for "Text Box"

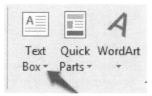

- Once you click on it, you will see "Text Box" options, just pick the first option which is "Simple Text Box"

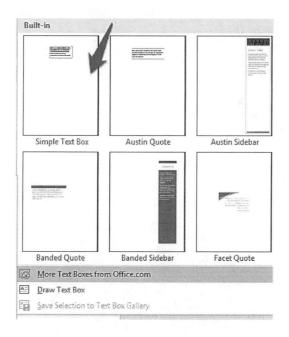

- Once selected, it will appear on your document with a bunch of texts telling you what "Text Box" is all about

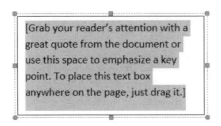

- Simply delete the highlighted instruction and insert your own words or number inside. Never forget that dots are used for resizing, it can be used to enlarge or reduce your "Text Box"

- You can also hide the lines in your "Text Box" by editing it, make sure your "Text Box" dots are still showing, look up, and select "Format". The "Format" tab only appears whenever any editable object is selected

- Then, under "Format", click on "Shape Outline" and select "No Outline", by default, your "Text Box" outline will be hidden

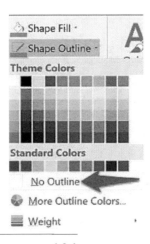

- Here is your result

- Then, click outside your "Text Box", you won't notice any line, as if the line never existed, whereas, it's still there but hidden. Whenever you click on the text, the dots will reflect that there is a "Text Box" on this text, you can also drag it as you were taught earlier by hovering on the dots at the edge, still, your mouse cursor shows plus (+) arrow, then you can drag and drop it in any area on your document.

Here is my Text Box

Drop Cap

Drop Cap is used to create a large format of text at the beginning of a paragraph

- To make use of "Drop Cap", simply highlight your text (a single letter)

A Word document is formatted to fit on a specific size page with the text automatically flowing om one page to the next. Excel supports printing, but its page breaks are not obvious, and because it's printing area can extend multiple pages horizontally as well as vertically the page breaks can be difficult to manage.

- Go to "Insert" in your menu bar

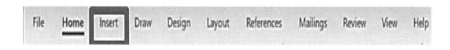

- Under the "Insert" tab, look for "Drop Cap" click on it

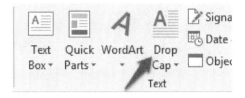

- Once you click on it, dropdown options will appear, select "Dropped" and your first letter at the beginning of your paragraph will receive the effect.

- **Note**: when it comes to "Drop Cap", if you highlight the first letter on the paragraph your mouse cursor is indicating, that is where your "Drop Cap" will take effect. Click outside the transformed text to make the dots and lines hidden.

A Word document is formatted to fit on a specific size page with the text automatically flowing from one page to the next. Excel supports printing, but its page breaks are not obvious, and because it's printing area can extend multiple pages horizontally as well as vertically the page breaks can be difficult to manage.

Watermarking for the Elegant Effect

Watermarking is a great way to show that a document requires special treatment without distracting from the content. How do we make use of Watermark? Simply follow these step-by-step procedures:

- Go to "Design"

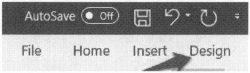

- Under the "Design" tab, look at your right-hand side, you will see the "Page Background" ribbon, above it, is the "Watermark" option, click on it.

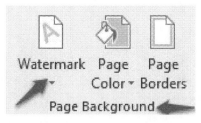

- Once you click on "Watermark", multiple options will be displayed, some are in diagonal format, and some are horizontal. Any template you click on will automatically reflect on your document. You can also customize your watermark. Select your preferred choice, or you choose "Custom Watermark" to customize your preferred choice

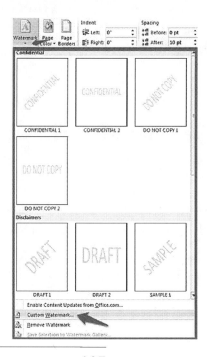

- Assuming we choose "Custom Watermark" by clicking on it, a dialog box will appear. There are three options to "Custom Watermark" which are: "No watermark", for no effect, "Picture watermark" for image effect, and "Text watermark" for text effect. Choose the preferred "Text" and "Language" you want to insert as well as "Font" format, "Size", "color" and "layout", once done, click the "Ok" button.

All the changes will automatically reflect on your document.

Putting Newspaper-Style Columns in a Document

- Go to the "Layout" tab

- Under the "Layout" tab, you will see the "Page setup" ribbon, within it you will also see your "Columns", click on it

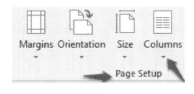

- You will see "Columns" dropdown options; let's pick "Three" because if you check any Newspaper, you will notice that on a page, the contents are normally divided into three columns.

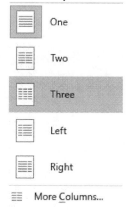

- Make sure you have content; else you won't see the effect of the "three" columns that you selected

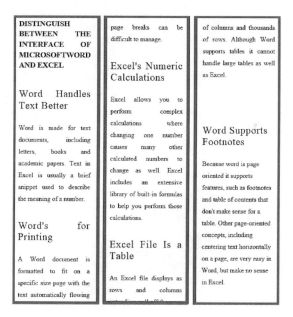

Landscape Document

It is important to note that a Word document can be in two formats which are "Portrait" and "Landscape". By default, your Word document is in "Portrait" format. How do we now switch between Portrait & Landscape?

- Simply go to "Layout"

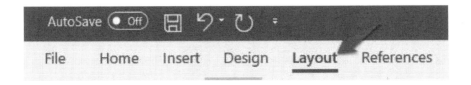

- Under "Layout", look for "Page Setup ribbon" select **Orientation**

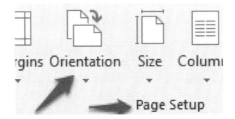

- You will see two options under "Orientation", which are "Portrait" & "Landscape". As I said earlier, a Word document by default is in "Portrait" (vertical format), once you switch it to "Landscape" as illustrated below, your presently opened Word document will be in horizontal shape.

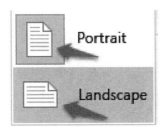

Printing on Different Paper Size

To print on a different paper size,

- Simply go to "Layout"

- Under "Layout", look for "Page Setup" ribbon, select "Size"

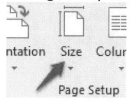

ntation   Size   Colur

Page Setup

- Under "Size", multiple options will be displayed. By default, your Word document paper size is on "A4", you can choose other options or click on "More Paper Sizes"

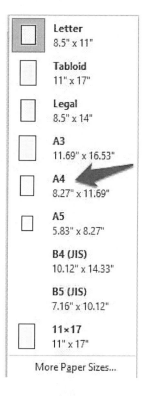

- Under "More Paper Sizes", you can set your paper "width" and "height" to your preferred taste, once you are done, press "Ok" to see the effect.

Showing Video in a Document

To show video in a document, follow these steps

- Go to "Insert"

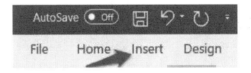

- Under the "Insert tab", on your right-hand side, you will see "Online Video Media", click on it

- A dropdown dialog box will appear with two options: "Online Video" which will refer you online (this requires your data connection) and "Video on My PC" (data connection not needed) which is the video from your PC storage. Once you choose your preferred choice you are good to go in watching your video through the Word environment

CHAPTER TEN

GETTING WORD'S HELP WITH OFFICE CHORES

Highlighting Parts of a Document

Highlighting parts of a document has been one of the quickest ways to perform your formatting tasks, such as bolding a text, increasing the font text size, changing text font, and other features. When it comes to effecting changes on some areas of your document content, the only option available is to highlight the parts of your document content.

How to Highlight a Text

There are only two ways of highlighting texts, which are: Mouse highlighting (click and drag) and Keyboard highlighting (Shift key + Navigation key).

Mouse highlighting (Click and drag)

- Place your mouse cursor at the beginning of your text area where you intend to start your highlighting from

Word is made for text documents, including letters, boo

usually a brief snippet used to describe the meaning of a

- Once your pointer has been placed at the beginning of where you want to highlight, simply right-click on your mouse and hold down (if you are using a desktop, which has an external mouse) or left-click on your mouse and hold down (if you are using a laptop which has an internal mouse), then, start dragging it to the last edge where you want to stop.

Word is made for text documents, including letters, books an

usually a brief snippet used to describe the meaning of a num

Keyboard highlighting (Shift key + Navigation key)

- Place your mouse cursor at the beginning of your text area where you intend to start your highlighting from

> Word is made for text documents, including letters, boo
>
> usually a brief snippet used to describe the meaning of a

- Once it is rightly positioned, hold down the "Shift" key on your keyboard and simultaneously press the "Navigation key" depending on the direction you want to navigate it. There are four Navigation keys, "Upward navigation", facing up; "Downward navigation", facing down; "Backward navigation", facing the back direction, and "Forward navigation" facing front. Below is an illustration of the "Shift" key together with the "Forward" navigation key

> Word is made for text documents, including letters, books an
>
> usually a brief snippet used to describe the meaning of a num!

Commenting on a Document

Commenting on a document is a great way of referring to it later and understanding your reason for particular tagged content.

Entering comments

- Select the content you want to comment on by highlighting it

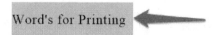

A Word document is formatted to fit on a specific size page with the text automatically flowing from one page to the next. Excel supports printing, but its page breaks are not obvious, and because it's printing area can extend multiple pages horizontally as well as vertically the page breaks can be difficult to manage.

- Once your text has been selected, simply go to the "Review" tab

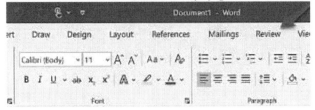

- Under the "Review" tab, you will see "New Comment" below it

- Enter "New Comment" by clicking on it, your highlighted text will be colored and another dialog box will appear on your right-hand side, the little "speech bubble rectangular shape" is a symbol or a referrer to your "comments box" at your left-hand side

Replying to comments

- Input your text inside the "Comment box", since our text is centered on "Printing", I will be typing "Printing Instruction", note below is another session to also "Reply" on your comment, just like an online post.

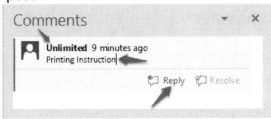

Note: don't be confused with the name "Unlimited" it is my PC name that I used, yours might not be "Unlimited", what your PC name is stored as is what will reflect on your comment session and your comment duration period after dropping your comment will be noted.

- You can reply on "Comment" with any word assuming I typed "More details on printing procedures" as my "Reply". Note that on a single comment, your "Reply" does not have limits.

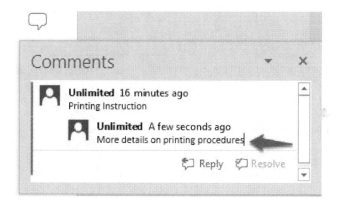

Resolving comments

- Highlight the comment or reply to be resolved or right-click on it to resolve it

Viewing and Displaying Comments

- Go to the "Review" tab

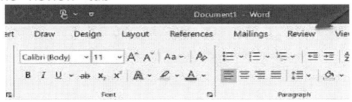

- You will see "Show Comments"

- Or on your document, you will notice a little speech rectangular icon, once you click on it, it will display your comments

- Your comment box will be displayed again for viewing or editing purpose

Tracking Changes to Documents

Keeping track of changes made to your documents is especially useful if the document is almost done, and you are working with others to make a revision or give feedback on your progress.

Working with Track Changes

- Simply go to "Review"

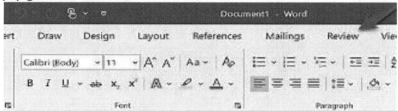

- Under "Review", at your right-hand side, you will see "Track Changes", click on it

- You will be given two options "Track Changes" & "Lock Tracking"

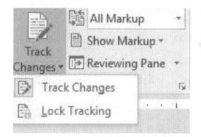

- Once you select "Track Changes", your content will be automatically monitored and tracked, and any changes made will be signaled with a red straight stroke as illustrated below with the additional words

A Word document is formatted to fit on a specific size page with the text automatically flowing from one page to the next. Excel supports printing, but its page breaks are not obvious, and because it's printing area can extend multiple pages horizontally as well as vertically the page breaks can be difficult to manage. Here is my additional input, kindly explain more further about printing

- You can also select "Lock Tracking" and a dialog box will appear requiring you to enter your "password" for prevention against unauthorized corrections which without the password, the other authors won't be able to add any changes.

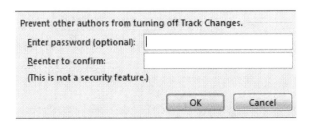

Reading and reviewing a document with revision marks

- Go to the "Review" tab

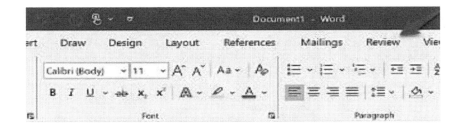

- Under the "Review" tab, at your right-hand side, you will see "Reviewing Pane", click on it

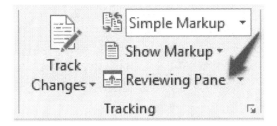

- Once you click on it, you will be given two options either to "Review Pane Vertically" or "Review Pane Horizontally". Assuming we choose "Review Pane Vertically", all your added words will be reviewed.

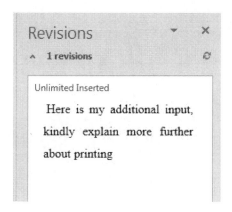

Marking changes when you forgot to turn on revision marks

- Go to "Review"

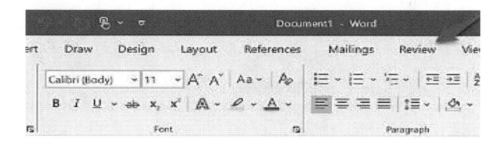

- Under the "Review" tab at your right-hand side, you will see "Sample Markup", click on it and select "All Markup"

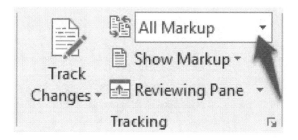

- Then, all your added texts will be marked with a red color and also underlined, as a way to make one know the added content from the one that was previously there before adding additional words.

Word's for Printing

A Word document is formatted to fit on a specific size page with the text automatically flowing from one page to the next. Excel supports printing, but its page breaks are not obvious, and because it's printing area can extend multiple pages horizontally as well as vertically the page breaks can be difficult to manage. Here is my additional input, kindly explain more further about printing

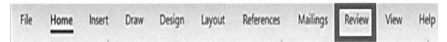

Accepting and rejecting changes to a document

- Simply go to "Review"

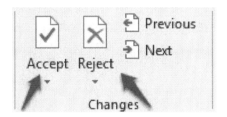

- Under "Review", at your right-hand side, you will see "Changes", above it is the "Accept" & "Reject" options

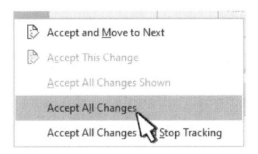

With the "Accept" option, you can move to the next track changes by selecting your preferred options under the "Accept" option

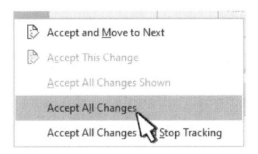

While the "Reject" option Undo changes and immediately moves to the next track changes. You can also select your preferred options under "Reject" just as in "Accept"

Printing an Address on an Envelope

- Go to "Mailings"

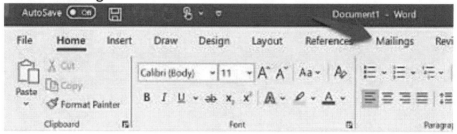

- Under the "Mailings" tab, at your left-hand side, you will see "Envelopes", click on it

- Simply fill in all the required details such as "Delivery address", "Return address", "Add to document" if need be. Once everything has been verified, click on "Print" |

Printing a Single Address Label (or a Page of the Same Label)

- Go to "Mailings"

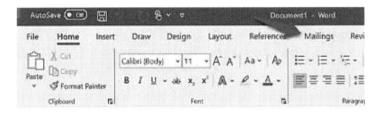

- Under "Mailings", on your left-hand side, you will see "Labels", click on it.

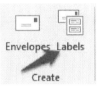

- Then, you can start filling the required input such as "Address", "Use return address" if need be (also select the amount of "Row" & "Column"), then click on your "Print" once you are done with labeling address.

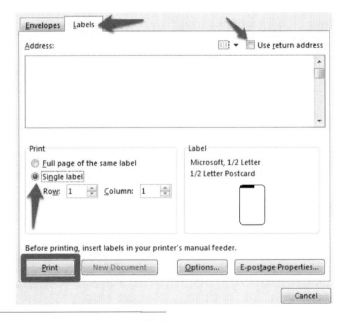

CHAPTER ELEVEN
KEYBOARD SHORTCUTS

Frequently used shortcuts

Ctrl + A	Highlight all your content
Ctrl + B	Applying bold to selected text
Ctrl + C	Copy content into the Clipboard
Ctrl + D	Font dialog box
Ctrl + E	Centralized text
Ctrl + F	Navigation for searching
Ctrl + G	Go to a page, section, line number
Ctrl + H	To replace a text
Ctrl + I	Applying italic to selected text
Ctrl + J	To justify your text
Ctrl + K	Insert hyperlink to content
Ctrl + L	Align text to the left
Ctrl + M	Move paragraph
Ctrl + N	Create a new document
Ctrl + O	Open a document
Ctrl + P	Print out document
Ctrl + R	Align text to the right
Ctrl + S	Save document
Ctrl + U	Applying underline to selected text
Ctrl + V	Paste the copied contents from the Clipboard
Ctrl + W	Close current document
Ctrl + X	Cut the selected content
Ctrl + Y	Redo the previous action
Ctrl + Z	Undo the previous action
Ctrl + [	Decrease the font size
Ctrl +]	Increase the font size
Esc	Cancel a command
Ctrl + Alt + S	Split the document Window
Ctrl + Alt + S	Remove the document Window split

Access Keys for ribbon tabs

Alt + Q	Move to the "Tell me" or Search field on the Ribbon to search for assistance or Help content
Alt + F	Open the **File page** to use Backstage view.
Alt + H	Open the **Home tab** to use common formatting commands, paragraph styles, and the Find tool.
Alt + N	Open the **Insert tab** to insert tables, pictures and shapes, headers, and text boxes.
Alt + G	Open the **Design tab** to use themes, colors, and effects, such as page borders.
Alt + P	Open the **Layout tab** to work with page margins, page orientation, indentation, and spacing.
Alt + S	Open the **References tab** to add a table of contents, footnotes, or a table of citations.
Alt + M	Open the **Mailings tab** to manage Mail, Merge tasks and to work with envelopes and labels.
Alt + R	Open the **Review tab** to use Spell Check, set proofing languages, and to track and review changes to your document.
Alt + W	Open the **View tab** to choose a document view or mode, such as Read Mode or Outline view. You can also set the zoom magnification and manage multiple document Windows.
Alt or F10	Select the **active tab** on the ribbon, and activate the access keys
Shift + Tab	Move the focus to commands on the ribbon.
Ctrl + Right arrow	Move between command groupings on the ribbon
Arrow keys	Move among the items on the Ribbon
Spacebar or Enter	Activate the selected button.
Alt + Down arrow key	Open the menu for the selected button

Down arrow key	When a menu or submenu is open, it's to move to the next command
Ctrl + F1	Expand or collapse the ribbon
Shift+F10	Open the context menu
Left arrow key	Move to the submenu when the main menu is open or selected

Navigate the document

Ctrl + Left arrow key	Move the cursor pointer one space at a time to the left
Ctrl + Right arrow key	Move the cursor pointer one space at a time to the right
Ctrl + Up arrow key	Move the cursor pointer up by one paragraph
Ctrl + Down arrow key	Move the cursor pointer down by one Paragraph
End	Move the cursor pointer to the end of the current line
Home	Move the cursor to the beginning of the current Line
Ctrl + Alt+ Page up	Move the cursor pointer to the top
Page down	Move the cursor pointer by scrolling the document down
Ctrl + Page down	Move your cursor pointer to the next page
Ctrl + Page up	Move your cursor to the previous page
Ctrl + End	Move your cursor to the end of the document

CHAPTER TWELVE
MICROSOFT WORD TIPS & TRICKS

Dark Mode

Do you know that you can turn on "dark mode" in Microsoft Word from the default background interface which is in white mode? The Dark mode is specifically designed for sight adjustment, majorly for the night users and other purposes.

To Enable Dark Mode

- Simply go to the top left-hand corner and click on your "File menu"

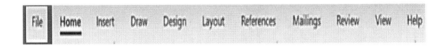

- Once you click on "File menu", scroll down, at the bottom left-hand corner, click on "Account"

- Once you click on "Account", you will see your "User Information", below it is "Office Theme" by default, it is on "Colorful theme", click on the little dropdown arrow as illustrated below to see other options, next on the dropdown list is "Dark Gray", let's select it and see its effect.

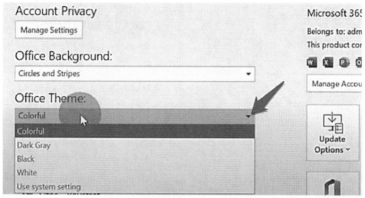

- "Dark Gray" makes your Word background interface a little bit dark

- You can select "Black" to get the "Dark mode" if you wish. Note that any change in your themes will also affect other Microsoft Suites such as Excel, PowerPoint, Outlook, and others.

- Here will be your Microsoft Word displayed interface

Changing the white document interface

Every of your theme settings or your customized theme settings can only affect the outlook, not the document content itself. To also change your white-board known as your document content area, simply follow these steps below:

- Go to your "Design tab"

- Under "Design", at your right-hand side, locate "Page Color" and click on it

- Then, you can select "Theme Colors" to "Black"

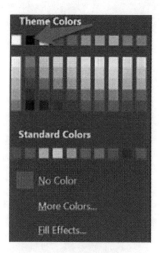

- Once you select "Color Black", your document content area will be on Black

Note: Your dark document content area has nothing to do with your printing out the document, it will print out your standard white format and black texts, your themes selection, and design document content, it only affects your Word interface not with the copies to be printed.

Turn Word Document into Interactive Web Page

- Go to the menu bar, and click on "File"

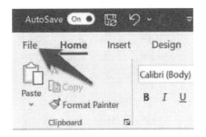

- Once you click on "File", scroll down and look for "Transform", once seen, click on it

- This will automatically open a pane at your right-hand side in your document where you can select any "Web Page" template of your choice

- Once you get your preferred choice, click on it and you will see the preview above

- Then, click on the "Transform" option to make changes

- You will be instructed about your preferred choice, that your document will be transformed to a Microsoft Sway web page. Once you are sure about your decision, simply click on "Transform" to proceed

- Once done, your web page transforming template will automatically open on your web browser

- You can also edit your web page by clicking on "Edit" which gives you the privilege to modify your web page template.

- You can also review the "Navigation"

- And also "Share" the link with others

Converting Photo or Text PDF into Editable Word Document

Convert from PDF with ease and edit your files without any restrictions, you can also do the same to an image text with Word 2019, you are limitless.

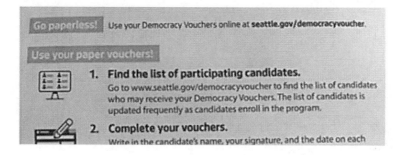

To see how this works;

- Simply go to the "File" menu

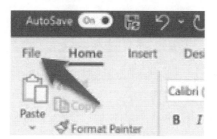

- In the "File" menu, a pane will appear by your left-hand side, click on "Open"

- At your right-hand side, "Open" features will appear, locate the document to be converted, whether an "Image text" or "PDF text"; if not found, navigate to where you have your file in your "Folders" to browse it or click and drag it into Word environment.

- You will get a "Microsoft Word Notification" that Word is about to convert your PDF to an editable Word document. The resulting Word document will be optimized to allow you to edit the text, so, it might not look exactly like the original PDF or Image-text especially if the original file contained lots of graphics. Note that for an effective result; make sure you have a data connection. Once you agree with the "Microsoft Word Notification" by pressing "Ok", then your PDF or Image-text will be displayed as an editable Word document

- Below will be your outcome, after the extraction of the text, which will be placed on your Word document for further self-editing.

Copy and Paste Multiple Items on Clipboard

Most of us are familiar with copy and paste but not aware of copying multiple texts differently and then see all your copied text while pasting it. Let me illustrate

- Assuming, I type "Copy me!", "Copy this!", and "Copy that!"

- Then, I copy it separately and I press "Ctrl + V" which is to paste, my result will only affect my last text which is "Copy that!"

Copy that!

- What if I want to paste the first text or the second text locally? Word will help with this by going to your "Home tab", below it, you will see your "Clipboard ribbon", there is a dropdown arrow indication, click on it to view all your different copied text

- Below is your outcome, where you can manually select the preferred text you want to paste by clicking on it, which in return will be pasted wherever your mouse cursor is pointing at (the blinking position).

Note: This is not limited to text, image also can be copied and pasted

Use formulas to calculate values

It is rarely known that Word performs mathematical calculations with different formulas like "Microsoft Excel", I will be showing you the possibilities

- Assuming, I have created my tabulated figures and all I need to do next is to sum it up without having to manually calculate it myself or with my PC calculator

Using formulas in Word
Word can do formulas too!

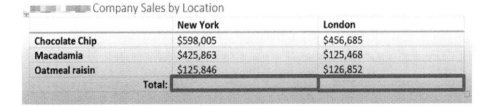

Company Sales by Location

	New York	London
Chocolate Chip	$598,005	$456,685
Macadamia	$425,863	$125,468
Oatmeal raisin	$125,846	$126,852
Total:		

- Look to the "menu bar" and select "Layout"

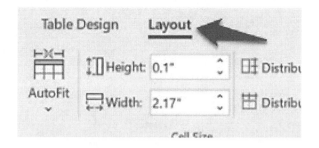

- Once selected, at your left-hand side, locate "Formula" and click on it

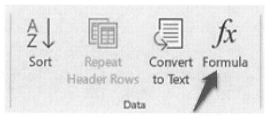

- Once you click it, a dialog box will appear where you can perform your arithmetic, this has been explained in "chapter seven", but for further understanding and the rareness of it. I have to show you more about it.

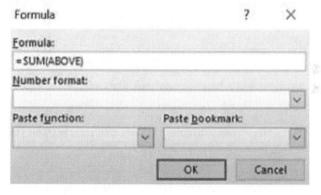

- Note, this is not only limited to summing up values, you can also click down below the illustrated apart and see all of the different formulas you can apply to your calculation. Calculating is not only about the summation of figures, other formulas can also perform other tasks such as getting your "Average" figure, "Max" for maximum figure, "Min" for minimum figure, and lots more, just scroll through the "scroll bar"

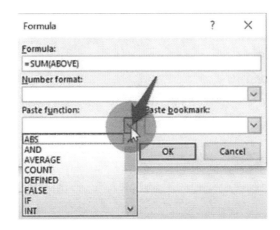

- I am going to stick to "=SUM(ABOVE)". To know more about what the symbols represent, kindly check back on "Chapter Seven" on the topic **"Using Math Formulas in Tables".** After you click on the formula you want, click "Ok" to see the effect

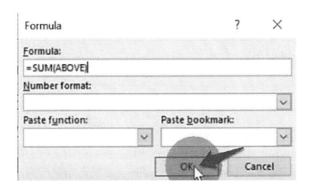

- Below is your total summation, make sure your cursor is on the cell where your total figure will be pasted, because if not you won't get your expected result

Sales by Location

	New York
	$598,005
	$425,863
	$125,846
Total:	$1,149,714.00

Assignment

From the table on pg. 241, calculate the total summation for "London" using the just explained procedure and do your manual calculation also for comparison.

Sort lists Alphabetically

- Do you know that you can sort lists in Microsoft Word and you can also sort lists in various ways? First of all, I will type some largest city in the World as illustrated below

Sort in Word

Tokyo
Lagos
Guangzhou
Istanbul
Karachi
Dhaka
Beijing
Mumbai
Shanghai
Delhi

- Secondly, the list will be automatically sorted out alphabetically. To do this, select (highlight) the list

Sort in Word

Tokyo
Lagos
Guangzhou
Istanbul
Karachi
Dhaka
Beijing
Mumbai
Shanghai
Delhi

- And then, go to your "Home tab"

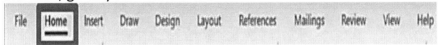

- At your right-hand side, click on the "Sort" icon which is represented with "upward A & downward Z with a downward arrow". After you click on it

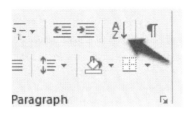

- A dialog box will appear titled "Sort Text"; make sure at your right-hand side you select "Paragraph", while at your left-hand side you select "Text", also click on the "Ascending" button for us to get our alphabetical order arrangement. Below it, you will see "My list has" which shows options, "Header row" and "No header row". For this illustration, I have no header row, which means I will click on "No header row". Once done, click on the "Ok" button.

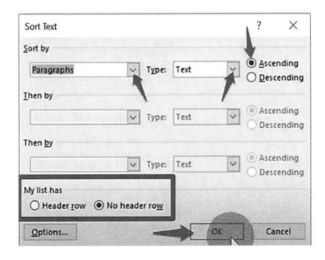

- You will notice your highlighted list will automatically rearrange itself alphabetically.

Sort in Word

Sort lists Numerically

Sorting out lists is not only limited to alphabetical arrangement alone, but you can also sort out lists numerically by following these steps:

- Highlight your numbers to be sort

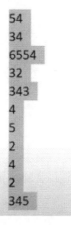

- Assuming, you want to rearrange the above numbers, simply go to your "Home tab"

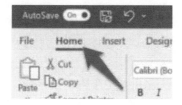

- At your right-hand side, click on the "Sort" icon which is represented with "upward A & downward Z with a downward arrow". After clicking it

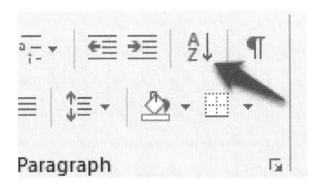

- A dialog box will appear titled "Sort Text", make sure at your right-hand side you select "Paragraph", while on your left-hand side you select "Number", also click on "Ascending" for us to get our numerical order arrangement. Below it, you will see "My list has" which shows options "Header row" and "No header row". For this illustration, I have no header row, which means I will click on "No header row", once done click "Ok".

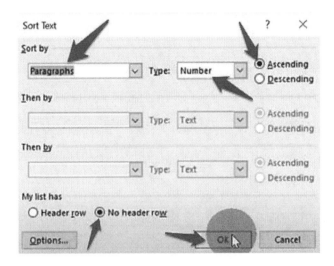

- You will notice your highlighted list will automatically rearrange itself numerically in ascending order.

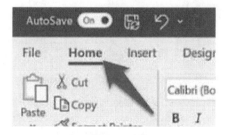

```
2
2
4
4
5
32
34
54
343
345
6554
```

Sort lists by Date

You can also sort out your listed dates in ascending order, without the use of Microsoft Excel. I know you are amazed by a lot of interesting Microsoft Word features. Now you understand, when I said, this is the right book you have purchased for your self-improvement. So, let us also see how sorting out dates works.

- Highlight your dates

2/15/1985
1/1/1929
5/4/1956

- To rearrange the above numbers, simply go to your "Home tab"

- At your right-hand side, click on the "Sort" icon which is represented with "upward A & downward Z with a downward arrow". After you click on it

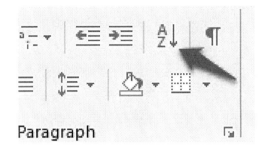

Paragraph

- A dialog box will appear titled "Sort Text", on your right-hand side, select "Paragraph", while on your left-hand side, select "Date". Also, click on "Ascending" for us to get our alphabetical order arrangement. Below, you will see "My list has", which shows options, "Header row" or "No header row". For this illustration, I have no header row, so, I will select "No header row". Once done, click on the "Ok" option.

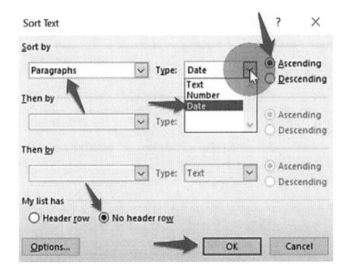

- You will notice that your highlighted date will automatically rearrange itself in an ascending way

1/1/1929

5/4/1956

2/15/1985

Collaborate with others via a link

Easily share your documents to work together with others as a team by using a link to send your document. In the past, if you wanted to work with others on a document, you have to email them by sending an attachment of your document for editing. They do the editing, send it back to you, and then, you have to merge all the edits which might consume a lot of time, especially when you are trying to see what has been added or removed; what a stressful process! Luckily, things have gotten a lot easier

- Simply look at the top right-hand corner of your Word 2019, you will see a "Share" option, click on it

- This opens a "share" dialog box which gives the access to share your document via a link. By default, it is on "Anyone with the link can edit"

- You can click on the default settings which is "Anyone with the link can edit", you will be shown other options such as "People in your domain with the link", "People with existing access", and "Specific people". Below are other functions you can tick or untick; "Allow editing", "Set expiration date" for termination of your shared link, "Set password" against unauthorized co-authors, you can also set "Block download" at your wish. Once you are through with your configuration, click on "Apply"

- If the above illustration is not what you need, press the "Cancel" option beside "Apply". After you click on apply, you will be brought here, type in the co-author email, you can also add some write-up with it, then send it, or you can also copy the link to your document depending on your preferred choice

Collaborate with others via mentioning someone's name

Easily share your documents to work together as a team with others by using "@" mentioning others to get their attention in responding to you as it is on your Facebook, whenever your name is mentioned, you are notified about it. To see how this works,

- highlight any part of your text document you want to inform others about

Easily share your documents to work together with others. @ mention others to get their attention.

- Then at the top corner of your right-hand side, click on "Comments"

- You see a dropdown option, click on "New Comment"

- Once you click on "New Comment", your highlighted text will be colored and another dialog box will appear at your right-hand side with your PC name or your Microsoft account name at the top of the "comment box"

- If you want to get someone's attention, simply start with an at "@" symbol, then you will be shown people within your list to be mentioned on your comment, which they are also going to be notified about

- Once you type or select the name of the person you want to add to your comment, you are going to be informed on granting access into your commented document by selecting either you "Share and notify" or "Don't share" button

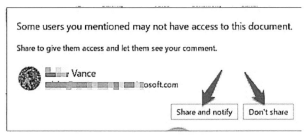

- Once you select "Share and notify", their names will appear at your comment session, then, you can now type what you want them to do about your comment when your notification reaches the other end

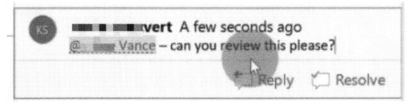

Pinning a Document

Another hidden feature on Word 2019 is the "pin" feature that enables you to quickly pin down a document and get back to the content in the future.

- To pin a document, simply go to "File menu"

- This brings us to the backstage within your "Home view"

- Look at your right-hand side, you will notice all your recently opened documents

- When you click on any of the recently opened documents, on your right-hand side, you will see two icons, the first one is the "share" icon which I have explained earlier, while the second one is the "pin" icon. Click on the "pin" icon to pin your preferred document

- Once you have clicked on "pin" to pin down your preferred document, simply click on the title "Pinned" to see your pinned document.

Rewrite suggestions

Another newly added feature of Microsoft Word 2019 is the "Rewrite Suggestions" which gives its subscribers access to rephrase words. Let's see how it works

- Assuming I typed the below sentence

I'm always working to continuously improve my videos.

- Now, you highlight the area which you want to rephrase. Let's assume it is "always working" in the above illustration

I'm always working to continuously improve my videos.

- Right-click on the selected text, a dialog box will appear, locate and click on "Rewrite Suggestions"

- Once you click on "Rewrite Suggestions", another dialog box will appear at your right-hand side with a suggestion of my highlighted text instead of "always working to" you can say "constantly working to" or "working all the time to"; I will click on "constantly working to"

- Then my highlighted text will be replaced with "constantly working to".

I'm **constantly working to** **continuously improve** my videos.

Assignment

Simply get another word replacement by using your "Rewrite suggestions" to rephrase "continuously improve" as illustrated below

I'm **constantly working** **to continuously improve** my videos.

Table of Contents

Microsoft Word has made it extremely easy to insert "table of contents"

- Simply go to the "References" tab

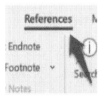

- Under "References", at your left-hand side, you will see your "Table of Contents", click on it

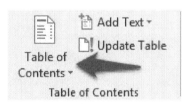

- Dropdown options of "Table of Contents" will appear where you can pick your preferred choice

Built-In

Automatic Table 1

Contents
Heading 1..1
  Heading 2...1
   Heading 3 1

Automatic Table 2

Table of Contents
Heading 1..1
  Heading 2...1
   Heading 3 1

Manual Table

Table of Contents
Type chapter title (level 1)..1
  Type chapter title (level 2)...2
   Type chapter title (level 3)..3
Type chapter title (level 1)..4
  Type chapter title (level 2)..5

- To customize your own "Table of Contents", make sure you first highlight your headings then, go to the "Home" tab and select your "heading style" on all your headings or titles, once done, position your cursor in your document area where you want your "Table of Contents" to appear on

- Then, you can go back to your "References" tab to select your preferred "Table of Contents" as illustrated earlier

Built-In

Automatic Table 1

Contents
Heading 1...1
  Heading 2...1
    Heading 3...1

Automatic Table 2

Table of Contents
Heading 1...1
  Heading 2...1
    Heading 3...1

Manual Table

Table of Contents
Type chapter title (level 1)...1
  Type chapter title (level 2)...2
    Type chapter title (level 3)...3
Type chapter title (level 1)...4
  Type chapter title (level 2)...5

- Then, your highlighted headings and selected heading style will enable your "table of contents" to display automatically. As you go through your document to add more words, some of your "Table of Contents" might change in numbering due to newly adjusted words

Contents
Dark Mode 1
Turn your Word document into an interactive web page 2
Convert Photo or Document PDF to an editable Word document............................... 3
Access your clipboard 4
Using formulas in Word 5

- You can keep your "Table of Contents" updated by clicking inside the top left-hand corner of your created "Table of Contents". A little displayed dialog box will popup named "Update Table"

- When you click on "Update Table", a dialog box will appear titled "Update Table of Contents", requesting you to select one of your preferred options between "Update page numbers only" and "Update entire table"

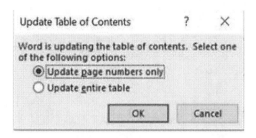

Citations and bibliography

Citation and bibliography on Microsoft Word are used to give credit to a source of information by citing the article, book, or other sources it comes from.

How to Insert Citation

To insert your citation, simply follow the steps below

- Firstly, construct a bunch of text to be cited

Citations
Insert and manage citations with ease.

Starting a cookie company just made sense. My charismatic personality served as a massive moat around the business. Plus, no one else could seem to replicate our cookie recipe.

Customers around the world started ordering cookies by the thousands. The response was humbling!

- Go to the "References" tab

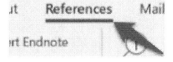

- At your right-hand side, locate "Insert Citation" and click on it

- Once you click on "Insert Citation", you will see dropdown options, choose "Add New Source" by also clicking on it

- Clicking on "Add New Source" will automatically open another dialog box titled "Create Source"

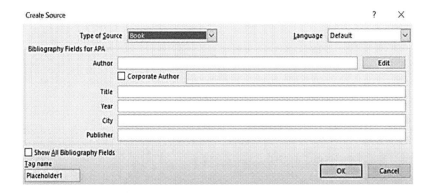

- Here, you can add all necessary information related to your source of information. For example, "Type of Source" will give you a dropdown of suggested lists to choose from about your citation, once you fill every required question, you can then click the "Ok" option

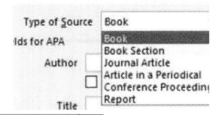

- Once you are done, your citation will automatically be added to your text

nality served as a massive moat

· cookie recipe, (Williams, 2025)

How to Create Bibliography

- To also create your bibliography, you can first get your "Style" format. Assuming, we choose the first option which is APA style

- Next, let also click on "Bibliography"

- A displayed dropdown list of "Bibliography" will appear, for understanding purpose, I will select "Works Cited"

- Then, your configured bibliography will appear below

Works Cited

Williams, J. (2025). *How the ▪▪▪ ▪▪▪ Company took over the food industry.* New York: Stratvert Publishing.

- You can also update subsequent citation by clicking on the "Bibliography" table and at your top left-hand corner, you will see "Update Citations and Bibliography"

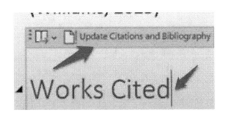

Conclusion

Wow, am glad you were able to make it through this practical guide on Word 2019. Now that you have gone through the process of learning, you can now see the power behind reading the right book. I believe you have no more worries about Word 2019 again.

I encourage you to also use this knowledge to contribute towards the wellbeing of humanity in your unique way, which in turn, your value will be appreciated in a greater way than you can ever imagine, how do I know this? This is the foundation of how Bill Gate, the founder of Microsoft started his pathway in life.

Can you compare before you went through this guide, and now after going through this guide? Now you fully understand what I meant by practical guide for all, irrespective of your career path.

Kindly, share with us your experience of this guide, looking forward to hear from you soon.

INDEX

23003389R00148